THE ADOLESCENT
OTHER CITIZENS
AND THEIR
HIGH SCHOOLS

THE ADOLESCENT OTHER CITIZENS AND THEIR HIGH SCHOOLS

A *Report to the Public and the Profession*

TASK FORCE '74
A National Task Force for High School Reform
John W. Porter, Chairman

ESTABLISHED BY THE CHARLES F. KETTERING FOUNDATION
THROUGH ITS EDUCATIONAL AFFILIATE
THE INSTITUTE FOR DEVELOPMENT OF EDUCATIONAL
ACTIVITIES, INC.

McGRAW-HILL BOOK COMPANY
New York   St. Louis   San Francisco   Düsseldorf
London   Mexico   Sydney   Toronto

Library of Congress Cataloging in Publication Data

Task Force '74.
 The adolescent, other citizens, and their high schools.

 1. Education, Secondary—United States. I. Title.
LA222.T34 1975 373.73 74-32110
ISBN 0-07-062918-8
ISBN 0-07-062920-X pbk.

1234567890 BPBP 798765

CONTENTS

List of Task Force Members... vii

Foreword... xi

Acknowledgments.. xiii

Introduction... xv

PART I: COMMUNITY INVOLVEMENT IN
EDUCATION: THE THIRD FORCE 1

Chapter 1: Reform Through Community
           Involvement: The Third Force..................... 3

Chapter 2: School Personnel and Their Response to
           Citizen Concerns.. 12

Chapter 3: Seven Approaches to
           Community Involvement............................. 21

PART II: WHO SHOULD CONTROL THE SCHOOLS? 33

Chapter 4: The Effect of Collective Bargaining on the
           Reform of Secondary Education 35

PART III: STUDENT RESPONSIBILITIES 43

Chapter 5: Identifying Student Responsibilities 45

Chapter 6: Educating for Responsibility Through the
            High School Curriculum 52

PART IV: ALTERNATIVE PROGRAMS AS
EDUCATIONAL OPTIONS WITHIN THE
FRAMEWORK OF THE LOCAL SCHOOL DISTRICT   63

Chapter 7: Alternative Programs as
            Educational Options 65

Chapter 8: Work/Study Programs as
            Educational Alternatives............................. 77

Chapter 9: Youth Service Programs as
            Educational Alternatives............................. 90

Chapter 10: Planning Processes for
             Alternative Programs 97

Chapter 11: Recommendations...................................... 109

Memoranda of Dissent 115

TASK FORCE '74
A National Task Force for High School Reform

B. FRANK BROWN

Director, Task Force '74
Director, Information and
Services Program
Institute for Development of
Educational Activities, Inc., the
Educational Affiliate of the
Charles F. Kettering Foundation
Melbourne, Florida

GEORGE L. BROWN

State Senator
Executive Director
Metro Denver Urban Coalition
Denver, Colorado

JOHN E. DOBBIN

Associate
Educational Testing Service
Atlanta, Georgia

DOROTHY M. FORD

Past National President
National Federation of Business
and Professional Women's Clubs
Whittier, California

STAFF OF TASK FORCE '74

W. Arthur Darling	Research and Writing Assistant
Phyllis H. Dexter	Secretary to Task Force '74
Linda J. Field	Report Coordinator
Emmat F. Frauman	Media Specialist
James R. Ryoland, Jr.	Administrative Assistant
Linda D. Schmitt	Assistant to the Secretary
Melba F. Smith	Office Manager

FOREWORD

In recent years, much attention has been focused on the function and future of the public high school in America. There has been more debate and polemic on this subject in the last year than at any time since 1959 when Dr. James Bryant Conant called for the preemption of secondary education by public comprehensive high schools.

Fifteen years of added experience with this model suggests the need for more than the unitary comprehensive high school. Change has been forced by a great increase in the proportion of graduates continuing to college, by mounting costs, and by demands for alternatives beyond the constraints of the traditional program, particularly for the 20 to 25 percent of American adolescents who fail to complete high school and for those others who are graduated without salable skills.

For most students, the American high school still performs efficiently and effectively in carrying out the four basic functions of the institution:

- It provides a useful place to be during the daytime from September to June.
- It socializes adolescents from different backgrounds as most students attend high schools outside their own neighborhoods.

• It offers a variety of programs directed toward college preparation, business, and industrial trades, in addition to special and general education.

• It tests, evaluates, and screens students for further education and for job opportunities with reasonable reliability.

The system of American secondary education based on the free public high school—now more than 100 years old—has provided instruction of higher quality to more students than any other educational system the world has ever known.

This does not answer the question, What next? To explore this question, and especially the issue of school governance and control—Who should decide what happens next?—the Kettering Foundation assembled Task Force '74.

The Task Force has, in its brief life span, attempted to place the questions and issues before the educational community and the public rather than to propose specific answers and solutions. It is within this framework and setting that the Task Force presents its final report which, hopefully, will not be "final" but will, indeed, generate ideas for consideration and directions for change and improvement in secondary education.

JOHN W. PORTER, *Chairman*

ACKNOWLEDGMENTS

The members of Task Force '74 acknowledge their indebtedness to the many educators, sociologists, students, and citizens at large who met with the Task Force to assist in its deliberations.

A note of gratitude is due those schools and school systems which welcomed visits by members of the Task Force or its professional staff.

A special note of appreciation is due Robert G. Chollar, president, Charles F. Kettering Foundation, and Samuel G. Sava, executive director, Institute for Development of Educational Activities, Inc., for funding the Task Force and allowing it to function as an autonomous body.

INTRODUCTION

In the course of the school year 1972–73, the National Commission on the Reform of Secondary Education conducted a broad study of the status of teaching and learning in the nation's high schools and made thirty-two recommendations for reform.

The Commission reported that structural supports of the nation's high schools were lacking in the areas of citizen involvement, programs to educate for responsible citizenship, and the management of alternative schools and alternative programs.

As an outgrowth of this study, the Charles F. Kettering Foundation established Task Force '74 to examine these three problem areas in depth and to make a report to the public and the profession.

During the school year 1973–74, the members of Task Force '74 traveled thousands of miles, visited schools, studied volumes of materials, heard numerous reports from many different consultants, and spent countless hours contemplating and debating the provocative issues raised by the three topics.

The Task Force concluded that the three issues are indeed vital and imperative to the process of reform. They are difficult areas because they are complex and rapidly developing. Yet, except for the debate on alternatives, none is receiving adequate attention.

The Task Force does not anticipate that its recommendations and suggestions will receive unanimous approval. It believes that this report will serve its purpose well if it can create a new awareness of the significance of the issues and stimulate further analysis.

The far-reaching recommendations contained in this report may suggest revolution—a quiet revolution, perhaps, but a real one. The Task Force members concluded that, unless many of the problems highlighted in this report receive high priority on our nation's work list, the vitality of our free public educational system will be in jeopardy. Though its members are not alarmists, the Task Force concluded that the democratic foundations of our country will be threatened if solutions to these problems are not found.

Within the lifetime of men still active:

• Mass communication, especially television, has destroyed the vitality of local and regional cultures, placing on the school greater burdens of acculturation to a vague, undefinable national ethic.

• The automobile and the national highway network have accentuated the rootlessness of an already restless society.

• Technology has changed people's perceptions of their relationship to their own work and increasingly separated the home from the job.

• Affluence has made children, and especially adolescents, consumers on a grand scale and thus subject as individuals to all the pressures of the consumer society.

• Family ties have weakened everywhere; and the home nexus from which students come—and to which they must return every evening—has become increasingly unstable and insecure.

The institution of the high school is not insulated from these changes in the larger society. Philip A. Cusick, writing in 1973, observed that most of us think of schools as places where the young go to learn how to work out their lives in a particular society. As such, schools are thought of not as settings for action and life, but as settings for preparation and training. For the students who inhabit them every day, however, schools are more than just training grounds. They are places where the business of life is actually being carried on; and the normal things students do at school reflect their immediate needs, expectations, and desires much more than their forecast of unspecified future events.

As the 1972 National Commission on the Reform of Secondary Education observed, despite a tempestuous history in which it had moved from crisis to crisis, the high school was ill-prepared for the widespread turbulence which began in 1968 with the first student demonstration at White Plains (New York) High School. During the four years that followed, American high schools were beset with student dissent, unrest, and racial discord. These events, coupled with countless court decisions restricting the authority of administrators, have radically changed the political atmosphere within the schools without changing their traditional mode of operation.

The Task Force believes that if educational reform at the high school level is to produce a better response to all students enrolled, certain principles will have to be accepted. These principles revolve around the following proposals:

- Citizens and parents must become more involved in the activities of high schools.
- Students must be informed of their rights and assured that such rights will be supported by due process procedures.
- Educating for responsibility must become a primary function of the school itself.

• Alternative programs to the traditional high school must be tested and established.

There are 15.2 million public high school students in grades 9 through 12 in America today, and among them are our future leaders. We need to do our best for them—for our sake as well as theirs.

THE ADOLESCENT
OTHER CITIZENS
AND THEIR
HIGH SCHOOLS

PART I

COMMUNITY INVOLVEMENT IN EDUCATION: THE THIRD FORCE

CHAPTER 1

Reform Through Community Involvement: The Third Force

Recommendation No. 1

The Task Force believes that most communities have individuals and groups who are interested in and have the potential for becoming actively involved in making decisions that affect the nature and future of education. Therefore, it is recommended that local citizens and community groups immediately increase their participation until they are actively involved in forming policies, making decisions, and governing their schools.

Recommendation No. 2

The Task Force recognizes that within a community a widely representative group should be formed to represent a broad mix of values, attitudes, and cultures. Group members should have the opportunity to increase their skills in communication, problem solving, and decision making. Therefore, it is recommended that each state develop methods of ensuring community involvement in all levels of education.

Recommendation No. 3

The Task Force realizes that some formal legal structure will be required if citizen groups are to be permanently established as a force in education. Therefore, it is recommended that each state develop methods to (a) enable community groups to develop and acquire skills in communication, problem solving, and decision making and (b) make available adequate funds to support community involvement in all levels of education.

Today's reform movement in secondary education had its beginnings in the late 1950s and early 1960s, during "the decade of innovation." The leaders of that decade were academicians and the forces behind their attempt were the large foundations and the federal government which plowed vast sums of money into a variety of new programs.

The process of reform through innovation failed for at least two reasons: (1) The innovative approach was piecemeal and the effort to change the high school involved manipulating only a part of the program rather than the total process. (2) Neither teachers, students, nor parents were involved sufficiently in the important decisions affecting the innovation. Educational innovators who were leading the movement took the position that innovation required expertise; suggestions from students and the public were likely to be irrelevant or even counterproductive.

Following the student upheavals of the late 1960s, the innovative efforts of the 1970s burgeoned into a total reform movement, and in recent years educators increasingly have involved students in efforts to effect change. But school officials have continued to overlook the most important component in high school reform—the force of the community.

If the high schools are to be significantly (
educators and students but members of the
must be involved in decision making and go
involvement in the schools is especially impo
education, because it has not happened be
have always been active at the elementary level; but citizen
participation in the high schools has usually been limited to
special interest groups such as band, parent, and athletic boost-
ers, and the involvement of the business community in business
courses or vocationally related programs.

Gradually, the institution of education has moved away from
the basic premise of democracy: that the people should control
their institutions. Education is the public institution closest to
the people. Citizens have the right to be involved in governance, policy making, and decisions affecting schools.

A Changing Society

Community involvement as a third force has been strengthened
by changes in the goals of American society. For a long time,
the dominant drive in society was toward growth and consumption. Now America is moving away from the growth and
consumption ethic, which has directed it for so long, and toward
an ecological and self-realization ethic.

A product of this change is dissent and conflict. During the
past decade, all aspects of the way our society functions have
been questioned. Mores are changing and new directions are
rapidly evolving. Against this background, the high school
finds itself perched precariously on the horns of a peculiar di-
lemma. The high school was created as an instrument of society
in a time of harmony and general consensus; it must now operate in a society which is characterized by confrontation, conflict, and dissension.

The high school as an institution must develop in consonance with a changing society. Since this new society is influenced by more diverse population groups than the old society, a much greater degree of citizen involvement will be required. Indeed, an important characteristic of the new self-realization ethic is emphasis on a participatory democracy through which people become a part of the decision-making process in their institutions. Educators increasingly must consult both the consumers of their services and those who finance these services before goals can be set or procedures developed for the institutions they administer.

Against this background, the most practical way to reform high school education and change public policy toward young people is through the increased involvement of citizens in their schools. To accomplish this goal, the involvement of citizens in education must take place in numerous ways and on a wide variety of fronts. The focus must be on citizens' efforts directed at all levels of decision making through a greater diversity of strategies.

Community Involvement Defined

Community involvement is defined by Task Force '74 as input from citizens to educational institutions in order to improve their functioning. The third force citizen involvement movement requires that information be received from citizens and introduced into the educational process to modify services, programs, and policies.

Citizen participation in schools has been a vague, elusive, cotton-candy term. To most people, it has meant attending PTA meetings, doing some volunteer activity at the schools, or being a member of an advisory committee.

In the 1970s, people are less interested in the advisory concept of participation in education. The key word is involvement, and citizens are concerned about having a voice in

policy formation, decision making, and school governance.
George Gallup was the first to point out the new mood of the
public in the *Second Annual Survey of the Public's Attitude
Toward the Public Schools*. Following this survey, taken in
1970, the Gallup polling organization drew this conclusion:

• The public has an appetite for more information about
the schools. It is important to tell the public about the schools,
but it also is incumbent upon the schools to listen to the public's view and, after serious examination, to take steps to meet
just criticisms.

Further observations on the need for citizen involvement in
education were made in late 1973 when the National Commission on the Reform of Secondary Education issued its report
and pointed out in one of its major recommendations that:

• Schools will not be able to achieve their purposes without increased help from people in the communities they serve.

An enormous amount of activity is now going on across the
nation to make the schools more responsive to their public and
their patrons. These efforts to make the schools responsive, like
any new movement, create chaos and unevenness. Some communities are moving rapidly. Others are still uninvolved. But
the movement is viable, growing, and becoming a force.

Despite what many sociologists say, citizen involvement in
decision making is a relatively new phenomenon going back no
more than four years. What makes it new is the change from
participation in an advisory way to actual involvement in
school governance.

Citizenship Redefined

Among the first results is a demand for a new definition of citizenship. Good citizenship, as taught in many civics classes of

the public schools, seems to require little more than voting and writing letters to congressmen. An effective democracy requires much more than marking ballots in periodic elections. Citizens must inform and affect government. Effective citizenship involves both a monitoring force and the assumption of responsibility to influence policies. It thus requires a more efficient two-way communication system between citizens and their government. The new definition of citizenship is "informed and active participation in public affairs in an ongoing manner."

Citizen involvement includes inquiries, requests, opinions, complaints, advice, suggestions, and volunteer productive activity.

Training for Citizenship

The Education Commission of the States pointed out in a recent workshop session that public school programs tend to emphasize one of two models in citizenship education:

1. Individualization of instruction so as to encourage optimum development of each individual, assuming that thereby each citizen will automatically be prepared to exercise his civic duty—the social, civic objective is approached indirectly.

2. A common program of subject matter and experiences considered essential, e.g., reading, national history, and literature, carried on to predetermined standards of achievement—the social, civic objective is approached directly, risking the possibility of indoctrination.

The first is obviously the model subscribed to by all leading professional organizations, but most schools actually pattern their training for citizenship after the second model. What is now emerging are new models embracing and going beyond both points of view.

The Third Force

To date, one of two disparate forces has controlled the major components of educational activity. First, through the era of emphasis on local control, came the district school board. Recently, the district board itself has come increasingly under the domination of the second force: the teacher organizations which are demanding a voice in everything that in any way relates (as most everything does) to the work of the teacher.

The third force, now emerging, is the consciousness of the community that it has a right to be involved. As a force, this group cannot be contained by rituals of parent and citizen participation to serve on advisory committees. Members of these groups insist that public control means what it says, that the public must have a genuine influence on the decisions that constitute governance in the schools.

What drives this new force is a sense that the high school is evolving into a self-perpetuating bureaucratic institution that exists separate from the individuals for whom it was created, by whom it is supported. The point is not that the school has become callous, but rather that as an institution it has become its own first priority.

The third force must be viewed as a movement for reform. Its members recognize that there will be no major changes in the high school until they can form a mass movement to answer the four important questions central to reform:

• Should we seek more and better of the same or must we rethink our view of education and its purposes?

• Should educational reform be undertaken primarily by professionals or primarily by the public?

• Should the educational process be continually open to public scrutiny in an ongoing manner?

• Should there be accountability for the education imparted to the children?

Professional educators are responsible for implementing policies determined by laymen. The public does not often exercise its right to state policies or evaluate procedures; only after the system begins to break down do the real issues come to the fore. Laymen have the right to call professionals to account for educational performance. Education is public business as well as professional business, and nobody ever intended that it become a professional monopoly. The third force insists that the scale not tip toward a technocracy where the public cannot exercise its right to scrutinize the professional process in education. The battlelines are being drawn.

The Task Force reached the conclusion that, if public education is to survive as a strong, viable institution, this third force must play a greatly increased role in policy formulation, decision making, and the governance of schools. To be effective, the third force must itself be institutionalized. *As a first step, state governments should form study commissions to examine the state constitutions and statutes for the purpose of removing all barriers to total community involvement in the schools.*

The Issues in Perspective

During the 1970s, many attempts have been made to change and reform education. These efforts have been spearheaded by educators. Now nonprofessional educators are assuming the vanguard of reform. The citizen advocate who unites with other like-minded citizens is a powerful force with which educational institutions must reckon. While advocacy is a relatively new kind of activity, it is becoming quite common.

Citizens' involvement is a way of bringing a new integrity to the school system. In no other way can the bureaucracy of the school be brought into step with the needs and aspirations of society.

Perhaps the most controversial of the many recent developments in education is the movement in large cities to give local communities control of their schools. The push toward community control arises out of the frustrations of minority groups. The lesson to be learned from these movements is that people who are increasingly frustrated with social institutions will increasingly struggle to control them or redirect them to better serve the needs of the people.

The high schools should operate as a cooperative venture between educators and members of the community which the schools serve. Citizens should be involved in governance and policy formulating, but the day-to-day decisions of operating the schools should remain with school administrators and teachers.

CHAPTER 2

School Personnel and Their Response to Citizen Concerns

Recommendation No. 4

The Task Force believes that significant educational change can be accomplished only through the cooperative efforts of educators, students, and citizens. Therefore, it is recommended that educators take the initiative in stimulating citizen involvement in high school reform.

The Task Force has called for civic group leadership in shifting from citizen participation to citizen involvement and for state governmental actions to stimulate the process. But educators themselves must play a significant role in creating mechanisms for involving citizens.

What has created the need for a greater response is a demand that the observations, judgments, and values of the community play an amplified role in the education of children and youth. The intent is to make the school system more responsive to what society requires. This in itself is a major reform.

The first cause of this new demand for community involvement in the schools is the public belief that the schools have failed to do the job for which they were designed—the teaching of skills which the society considers basic.

Since the authority of school administration is derived from the people, the ultimate responsibility is to the people. As the interest of citizens in their institutions moves beyond the vote, school administrators must make a mighty effort to achieve the fullest possible citizen involvement. Citizens should be active in their schools as planners, advisers, volunteers, advocates, and decision makers. The response that communities now want from school officials is the opportunity for this kind of involvement.

As a school or school system moves toward the development of new mechanisms to respond to citizen concerns, there are a few basic principles which should be observed:

1. The role in which the citizen is to be involved must be carefully defined.
2. Sufficient information must be available to the citizen participant to enable him or her to make decisions wisely.
3. The viewpoints of all segments of the community must be represented in the cooperative decision-making process.

While nobody can offer a perfect definition of quality education, quality will be improved in the minds of the people when there is serious and effective community involvement. There is also considerable evidence, despite testimony to the contrary by leaders of their associations, that teachers react favorably to purposeful citizen involvement.

School administrators must recognize that any significant change or reform can be wrought more easily with the serious involvement of citizens. Without their assistance, even minor changes can cause enormous problems. The mood of many communities is such that, unless school administrators seize the initiative and invite citizen involvement, they may soon find themselves faced with increasing numbers of adversary groups demanding changes.

Measuring Involvement

The Task Force suggests use of the Arnstein "Ladder of Citizen Participation" by educational policy makers and planners in developing mechanisms appropriate to the different degrees of community involvement as well as ways to identify activities that frustrate such involvement.

Types of Participation and "Nonparticipation"

Arnstein posits a typology of eight *levels* of participation. [The top three levels are accepted by the Task Force as citizen *involvement* rather than mere *participation*.] For illustrative purposes the eight types are arranged in a ladder pattern, each rung corresponding to a measurement of citizens' power in determining the end product.

The bottom rungs of the ladder are (1) *Manipulation* and (2) *Therapy*. These two rungs describe levels of "nonparticipation" that have been contrived by leadership to substitute for genuine participation. Their real objective is not to enable people to participate in planning or conducting programs, but to enable powerholders to "educate" or "cure" the participants. Rungs 3 and 4 progress to levels of "tokenism" that allow the have-nots to hear and to have a voice: (3) *Informing* and (4) *Consultation*. When they are proffered by powerholders as the total extent of participation, citizens may indeed hear and be heard. But under these conditions they lack the power to ensure that their views will be *heeded* by the powerful. When participation is restricted to these levels, there is no follow-through, no "muscle," hence no assurance of changing the status quo. Rung (5) *Placation* is simply a higher level tokenism because the ground rules allow have-nots to advise, but retain for the powerholders the continued right to decide.

Further up the ladder are levels of citizen power with increasing degrees of decision-making clout. Citizens can enter into a (6) *Partnership* that enables them to negotiate and engage in trade-offs with traditional powerholders. At the topmost rungs, (7) *Delegated Power* and (8) *Citizen Control,* citizens obtain the majority of decision-making seats, or full managerial power.

Obviously, the eight-rung ladder is a simplification, but it helps to illustrate the point that many have missed—that there are significant gradations of citizen participation. . . .[1]

8 | Citizen control
7 | Delegated power
6 | Partnership

Degrees of citizen power

5 | Placation
4 | Consultation
3 | Informing

Degrees of tokenism

2 | Therapy
1 | Manipulation

Nonparticipation

EIGHT RUNGS ON A LADDER OF CITIZEN PARTICIPATION

While Arnstein's ladder was developed from federal programs of involvement such as urban renewal and model cities, it is equally appropriate to citizen participation in the high school community.

Principles that Facilitate
Community Involvement in Schools

In addition to Arnstein's ladder, there are other guidelines which lead to the successful involvement of citizens in their schools. These have been identified by the Task Force as follows:

• Early success from citizen participation reinforces involvement and commitment.

• Policies and actions will more likely be successful and lasting when they are democratically developed and implemented.

• Involvement is enhanced when all people feel that they have an equal opportunity to influence the group and participate in leadership.

• Involvement will be greater and more productive when work is done in intimate, informal, primary groups with the objective, systematic truth-seeking.

• Community response will vary according to the degree of citizen involvement in study, planning, and action groups. All groups must be representative of a "mix" of people living in a community—all ideas and interests must be considered.

• The joining of new skills in communication, problem solving, and decision making increases citizen interest and involvement.

• People become more involved and committed when they have an opportunity to evaluate and reevaluate their objectives, methods, activities, and programs.

• It must be recognized that initiative rests with the people—decisions are made by them out of their knowledge and convictions.

• Objectives must grow out of a local situation and begin with conditions as they are—specific interests, concerns, and problems.

Citizen Concerns

The Task Force believes that educators have inadvertently alienated citizens because they are too absorbed in their own day-to-day problems. Before the goal of citizen involvement can be achieved, educators and citizens must jointly overcome the old problem of citizen alienation.

Within the last few years, many high schools have grown enormously in size. As the school's student population increased, its internal problems multiplied almost in direct proportion. School administrators have had little time to consider such intricate problems as citizen involvement. The result is a growing feeling in communities everywhere that the schools are distant, unresponsive, and isolated from reality.

The separation of citizens from the school system is not a local, but a national phenomenon. Citizens everywhere have become estranged by educational paternalism and by union contracts which tend to ignore parental concerns. The result is that many people now view the schools as unresponsive—even hostile. As a consequence, citizens are underrepresented in the governance of an institution which was designed for their participation. Among the chief causes of this breach between citizens and their schools are:

1. Parents and citizens are confused by the growing complexity of the school system.

2. There are often no avenues by which citizens can register grievances.

3. Many educators are overly defensive in their responses to grievances when they are brought forward.

4. Taxpayers have been alienated by the growth of the budget.

5. Increasing problems of vandalism and crime in the schools have led to a cynical view of the educational enterprise.

In the face of rapidly growing citizen alienation, a number of practices should be introduced at once to improve the responsiveness of the schools.

The great need is for an increase in communication from the citizen to the schools in order to overcome public frustration. Such communications from citizens may assume two forms: (1) general communications including requests, inquiries, and complaints and (2) involvement communications which include monitoring, advice on governance, and volunteer activity.

A great part of the responsibility for involving citizens lies with the local school administrator and the school board. They should provide the leadership necessary to bring about a viable community involvement program to their constituency. Because of the present disaffection which so many people feel for the schools, such efforts are now a matter of the highest priority. What is required is considerable skill and knowledge about the taxonomy of citizen involvement.

Constraints to Public Involvement in School Affairs

Even in communities where some people demand involvement with their schools, most people avoid participation. Whether from alienation or apathy, they have resigned themselves to the unresponsiveness of schools. This hesitancy takes a variety of forms. Members of the Task Force compiled a list of some of the most "popular" reasons, excuses, and explanations why people refuse to become involved:

ALIENATION	APATHY
Community domination by professional educators	Belief that educators know best; they are intelligent and have had professional training
Educators' disbelief in ability of community to make "right" decisions	A community feeling that citizens are not wanted or needed
No mechanism available by which a person can affect the way a school operates	Community roles that conflict with school involvement, i.e., taxpayer association memberships, large landowner, etc.
It is only a formality; educators do not really listen to parents	Takes too much time for amount accomplished
A parent's voice is muffled by the interpretation put on it by the educator and by technical language	Economically poor environment—survival is the primary concern
Clever and subtle (PR slick approach) manipulation of public by educators	Don't know anything about school affairs or lack of interest in school program
Open disagreement with school personnel will reflect on teacher/administration attitudes toward own children in school, their grades, advancement, and recommendations	No children involved in the school program, thus no personal commitment
	No transportation available to them
Legal barriers to involvement	Belief that their children do not want them to participate

Educators must deal honestly and effectively with these root causes of neglect.

NOTE

1. Sherry R. Arnstein, "A Ladder of Citizen Participation," *AIP Journal*, July 1969, vol. 35, no. 4, p. 217. (Reprinted by permission of the author and the *Journal of the American Institute of Planners*.)

CHAPTER 3

Seven Approaches to Community Involvement

Recommendation No. 5

The Task Force endorses the idea of community school boards for individual schools. Therefore, it is recommended that individual community boards be permitted to participate in the selection of principals, the evaluation of teachers, authorization of programs of instruction, approval of local building plans, etc., within centrally approved budgets. The school district board should therefore be limited to general policy formation, budget preparation, and review.

Recommendation No. 6

The Task Force recognizes that advisory committees must be trained before they can become involved effectively, but insists that this training must not come from the groups or professions which are being advised. Therefore, it is recommended that funds be allocated for external trainers and staff assistants not paid or controlled by local school boards. or administrators.

Recommendation No. 7

The Task Force applauds the involvement of business and industry in the education of the nation's youth and seeks its extension. Therefore, it is recommended that the business community accept increased responsibility for helping educators find solutions to some of the problems of the high school.

This report described in Chapter 2 the need for school personnel to encourage more citizen involvement. This chapter discusses various approaches that can be used by school personnel for such purposes. How the task is accomplished will vary from community to community, but there are a number of common strategies by which citizens can become involved in efforts to bring about reform.

These various approaches do not necessarily come in any particular order, nor are they mutually exclusive. For example, advocacy groups often borrow strategies from ombudsmen and consumer groups, and vice versa. It is not unusual to find more than one approach employed at the same time in a given community. The techniques most often used are advocacy, consumer, ombudsman, citizen, business community, and PTA.

The Advocacy Strategy

The advocacy approach responds to the failure of institutions—in this case, the schools—to do what they are mandated to do by law and public policy. Built into the advocacy model is an instinctive mistrust of any kind of bureaucracy that is not under constant public scrutiny. Advocacy should be seen as intervention on behalf of consumers with the institution and the administrative functions which are affecting their lives. The purpose is to bridge the gap between consumers and the bureaucracy. The focus is on promoting the welfare of the individual as a means to accomplish the ends of reform, constantly asking the questions: Why do we have these problems? What can we do to deal with them?

The advocacy model is effective only for certain kinds of reform issues. It can deal efficiently with issues which are precise, well defined, and manageable. Furthermore, the advocacy model is not appropriate to address pervasive failures for which there are no specific remedies.

Among the reasons for the rise of advocacy is the tendency of institutions to put the blame for failure on the very people whom they have failed to serve—explaining bad reading scores by the presumed incapacity of the children, punishing truant children by suspending them from school. The latter, which has been a common practice, is a consummate irony that expresses the failure of the institution to respond effectively to its consumers.[1]

In its efforts for reform, the advocacy model uses three basic techniques—administrative negotiations, litigation, and legislation. A series of strategies for advocacy groups is proposed by sociologist Larry Brown, director of the Massachusetts Advocacy Center in Boston.

• The first strategy is to make the issue a public one. The necessary first step is to gather hard data on a problem, with thorough documentation: the media will accept a school report as legitimate even when it is not fully documented but will demand evidence from an advocacy group.

• The second strategy of the advocacy model is to get the issue before the media and keep it there to apply pressure on state and local officials to negotiate. Advocacy groups should operate and negotiate in good faith without hidden agendas.

• The third strategy is to go over the head of the administrators responsible for the agency—or around them—to another government agency.

• The fourth strategy is the threat of litigation.

• The fifth strategy is the threat of organizing a coalition of parent groups and organizations to heat up the issue.[2]

The Consumer Strategy

The consumer approach was largely developed and made popular through the activity of Ralph Nader. This is the technique of an active citizen who knows how to prosecute a complaint—his own or a third party's.

Actually, the consumer approach calls for a redefinition of citizenship beyond the civics textbook notion of citizenship, beyond voting and obeying the law, and paying taxes. The new definition of citizenship includes having knowledge about how to prosecute a complaint, producing citizens' handbooks, intervening in proceedings, scrutinizing laws that are passed, and evaluating legislators.

While this strategy was originally product oriented, it has proved an effective mechanism for involving citizens, especially young people, in the process of change and reform in education.

The consumer approach has developed the following roles for citizens:

1. *Complaint handling.* People of all ages, including both teen-agers and retired persons, are trained to prosecute consumer complaints effectively.

2. *The citizen as an intervener.* Citizens are trained to intervene effectively in proceedings from school board meetings to legislative committee hearings.

3. *The citizen as an investigator.* The focus here is on the citizen's right to know both the applicable law and the details of current practice.

4. *The citizen as a litigator.* This embraces the instigation

of lawsuits; a necessary first step may be persuading attorneys
to contribute their services to a worthy cause.

5. *The citizen as an advocate.* Performing this role, which
pervades all the others, requires training in how to present
points of view.

6. *The citizen as a monitor.* This includes a constant review of policies, rules, regulations, and laws.

7. *The citizen as a lobbyist.* This involves persuading an
administrator or legislator to the consumer's point of view.

Much of the success of the practitioners of the consumer approach grows from their insistence that people who are not experts on a particular subject can be effective in redressing a
grievance.

Part of the consumer strategy is to magnify activity through
the media. Use of the consumer model requires training citizens in the design of tactics that will attract the attention of
the media.

The Ombudsman Strategy

The word "ombudsman" is Scandinavian and refers to a commissioner appointed by a king to hear and investigate complaints by private citizens against government officials or
agencies. The Americanized version quite often applies to education and refers to an officer appointed by the school board to
cope with complaints from students and parents against the
school or its practices. He may operate at either the school district or individual school level. The various action lines and hot
lines set up in communities to service students or adults are
forms of the ombudsman technique.

The school ombudsman approach differs from other citizen
involvement processes in that it seeks solutions within the system as it exists. This approach does not threaten orderly pro-

cess and speaks to the needs of the individual rather than those of the community.

Ombudsmen are used by schools and school systems in a variety of ways. Among the purposes that can be served is the recruitment of representatives from the community to work with and in the schools: the ombudsman role is often attractive to leaders of civic groups.

The ombudsman necessarily suffers from divided loyalties: he is appointed by the school system, his responsibility is to the person represented. When the needs of the institution and the interests of the individual run counter to each other, the ombudsman tends to lose credibility on one side—or both. Ombudsmen should commit themselves to roles as advocates for the students and the community. Their major function should be intervention, not the maintenance of what may be unsatisfactory official procedure or policy.

Community School Boards for Individual Schools

The original theory behind the institution of the school board was the twofold notion that lay people should control education and that they should function as delegated (usually elected) representatives of the entire community. An insurmountable problem of the modern school board as an effective vehicle of citizen involvement is the growth in size of school districts, particularly in urban areas where it is not uncommon to find over a hundred schools housing several hundred thousand youngsters and operating with a school budget of many millions of dollars. The operation is simply too large and unwieldy to allow for effective citizen involvement. Under this system the whole theory of lay control of education breaks down, as it is impossible for one school board made up of five to ten school board members to represent adequately the disparate elements of a large urban community.

Another factor contributing to the remoteness of school boards is the consolidation of previously independent districts. As consolidation has reduced the number of districts enormously, fewer school board members are called upon to represent more and more people scattered over ever-growing territory, and citizens are pushed farther from the decision-making process.

In order to solve the twin problems of decentralization and citizen involvement, a few of the larger urban school districts have instituted a separate community school board for each school within the system. The most frequently cited model is the Louisville, Kentucky system. The purposes of the Louisville plan are to overcome the hostility of a highly diversified inner-city minority population who believe that the central school board is insensitive to their needs and to set up a collaborative decision-making process. In the words of Superintendent Newman Walker:

> What we are doing is attempting to find the best ways by which dialogue and negotiation can continually take place between all of the divisive constituencies of the school system.[3]

In Louisville, parents of children at an individual school make up the majority of the local school's board, but community representatives other than parents are included. All boards for high schools include students, and some of the elementary school boards have student members from the elementary level.

If individual school boards are to succeed, citizens must be allowed involvement in significant decisions affecting the operation of the schools. Great care must be taken to assure that school boards do not become instruments of legitimation for educators rather than decision makers on their own authority. Most of the central boards have been reluctant to delegate power and have restricted the individual school boards to advisory functions. The best governance model for individual school boards includes the involvement of parents and citizens from the community selected by the community, teachers selected by the teachers themselves, and students selected by students, with the school administrator serving ex officio.

In making its observations about school boards for individual schools, the Task Force noted particularly that trust between the professional and lay communities was greatly strengthened by the process of collaborative decision making.

Citizen Advisory Committees

Very close to the concept of school boards for individual schools is the proposal for citizen advisory committees in education. These committees are proliferating, and most of them function in much the same manner as a school board for an individual school.

Evidence of the strength of the third force movement may be seen in the fact that a number of state legislatures have on their agenda items relating to the involvement of citizens in education. The Florida Legislature in 1973 passed a law which specifically mandated all school districts within that state to involve parents, nonparent members of the community, students, and teachers in the operation of the schools. The only choice left to school systems was whether they set up these advisory committees on a district or individual school basis. Many school systems have opted for advisory committees for each school.

In the Florida plan, each advisory committee has a minimum membership of seven, and details of its composition are determined by the local school board. Some school systems are electing the committee members while others mandate appointment by the school principal after a call for volunteers.

The intent of the Florida legislation is to increase the accountability of the school staff and the school board to the community which it serves.

While the Task Force questions whether the concept of citizen advisory committees goes far enough, these boards are highly significant. They mark the end of a "hands off" education era for parents and citizens and the beginning of a new era of citizen involvement in educational decisions. One of the causes of the present trouble in the schools is that educators have gone it alone with scant regard for the involvement of parents and citizens. As a consequence, educators have received outside opinions only on the most controversial issues. Advisory committees will provide a stream of new inputs.

As a scheme for facilitating citizen involvement, the advisory committee is viable only when its members participate in decision making. Too often they merely react to decisions taken by others. The function of advisory committees ranges from token recognition to total governance, depending on the interpretation of the rules by the members of the committee and the school administrator involved.

One of the problems with the concept of advisory committees seems to be the very word "advisory." Educators interpret this term literally as meaning "to make suggestions," while citizens interpret it as "to make recommendations"— which they expect will be heeded. The very use of the word advisory, commonly adopted as a compromise between legislators and the professionals, puts the concept at a disadvantage. This problem can be resolved by changing the name from advisory committee to monitoring commission, the name given by the courts to the committees the judiciary sets up in court-ordered desegregation procedures.

A successful advisory committee has two components: (1) a very clear charge as to the committee's functions and (2) sufficient power to make its service worthwhile. Advisory authority should consist of both veto power and involvement in policy-making decisions.

Parent Teacher Association

An organization with great potential for increasing citizen involvement in the schools is the PTA. Traditionally, the PTA bent over backwards to keep from becoming involved in decision making or school policies. Before 1972, PTA bylaws commanded that the organization cooperate with the schools in ways that will "not interfere with administration of the schools and shall not seek to control their policies." Now the bylaws require that the organization "seek to participate in the decision-making process establishing school policy."

In their discussion with teachers' union leaders, the members of the Task Force were surprised at the resentment expressed against the PTA for what the leaders described as "using teachers." The charge was made that many PTA's put pressure on a principal to compel teachers to join the PTA and attend meetings. In the words of David Selden, former president of the American Federation of Teachers, "What is most needed is to take the 'T' out of PTA." In New York, where the union is strongest, PTA has never taken root; and a rival organization, United Parents Association, performs similar functions. The Task Force recommends the New York situation as a national model: the PTA should become an association of *parents taking action.*

The Business Component

Businessmen and their organizations have long been the educational institution's silent supporters, available for donations of money, equipment, and even personnel. Now business is finding that its languorous involvement gained it few benefits. Many of today's high school graduates are so ill-equipped with basic skills that large companies have been forced to set up training programs of their own at considerable cost. Business and industry are now prepared to assume more active roles in the schools.

Many companies, under urging from the United States Chamber of Commerce, have begun to become involved in local high school programs. Schools and business are learning to cooperate, both sides modifying previous expectations and sharing programs and services for youth. There must be a true sharing of responsibility for planning, implementing, and evaluating what the schools do for students who must—or wish to—acquire salable skills in high school. Both parties must work together in developing curricula, in using community and business facilities, in arranging for representatives of business to help teach adolescents, and in career counseling. Business needs better-trained employees; students and teachers need greater understanding of commerce and enterprise.

NOTES

1. See William Ryan, *Blaming the Victim* (New York: Pantheon Books, 1971).

2. Excerpt of remarks made by J. Larry Brown, director, Massachusetts Advocacy Center, Boston, Massachusetts, to members of Task Force '74 at a meeting in Boston on April 8, 1974.

3. Statement made by Newman Walker, superintendent of schools, Louisville, Kentucky, to members of Task Force '74 at a meeting in Louisville on December 17, 1973.

PART II

WHO SHOULD CONTROL THE SCHOOLS?

CHAPTER 4

The Effect of Collective Bargaining on the Reform of Secondary Education

Recommendation No. 8

The Task Force is aware that there are many decisions which can only be made after completion of negotiations between teacher organizations and school boards, but cautions against the further extension of collective bargaining into areas over which citizens have traditionally exercised control. Therefore, it is recommended that collective bargaining between school boards and teachers be limited to the area of teacher welfare, i.e., salaries, fringe benefits, and grievance procedures.

Recommendation No. 9

The Task Force believes that citizen concern about the privacy of school negotiations which tends to prevent their in-

volvement in many of the negotiated decisions is legitimate and, hopefully, such negotiations will be more open to public review. Therefore, it is recommended that upon the completion of privately conducted negotiations—but prior to the signing of any collective-bargaining agreement—the school board should be required to hold a series of public hearings to allow maximum citizen input before final contract approval.

Recommendation No. 10
The Task Force notes that salary arrangements for middle management are now tied too closely to teachers' salaries, creating a lock-step ratio in salary schedules for teachers and principals. Therefore, it is recommended that school boards recognize the complexities and extreme pressures of the principalship and designate principals and other middle-management groups as members of the management team with compensation determined independently.

Within the past few years, teacher organizations have expanded and strengthened to the point where they are gaining control over many elements of school operation. Unquestionably, teacher organizations have become a powerful second force in the operation of our schools.

The word "our" in the phrase "our schools" is the key consideration here. In a democracy, the schools should be the joint responsibility of the public and the professional staff which operate them. But, as the high schools come under the influence of collective bargaining, there is growing question as to whether the interests of citizens and the needs of students will be appropriately addressed. A bureaucracy absorbed in dealing with the demands of its employees cannot pay much attention to students or citizens. The public is put in the role of petitioner and begins to view the educational bureaucracy as distant and unresponsive.

When the bureaucracy and the teacher organizations form an alliance, the public is told that all the problems of the schools can be solved by money. School budgets skyrocket—in some places, the Task Force was told the rise has been in excess of 100 percent within the last decade. The public pays for a system that does not improve, over which the citizen-elected school board seems to have steadily diminishing authority.

The fundamental political premise in a democracy is that the people control their institutions. Today's big-city school systems, which must be run according to the rule book of the collective-bargaining contract, have wandered far from that premise.

Collective bargaining as an "effective force" goes back only to 1965 when Michigan enacted the first strong law favoring bargaining between school districts and their teachers. Today, thirty-seven states permit some type of bargaining by school boards. Through strikes and threats of strikes, teachers in the large cities have acquired policy-setting powers rivaling those of the school board.

The Task Force recognizes that the rights of teachers can and should be safeguarded by teacher organizations. Consequently, this report does not oppose collective bargaining, negotiation, or the right of teachers to strike in states where strikes are legal. The Task Force does urge, however, that the areas that may be covered by collective-bargaining contracts be limited by law to assure the community is not disenfranchised and students' needs are not neglected.

Problems for the Local Board

Labor negotiations are expensive to a school district. Some large districts can afford to hire labor relations experts, but many small districts cannot even assign a staff member to full-time duty in this area. Meanwhile, local teacher organizations obtain highly professional guidance from their state associations and national organizations. The local teacher group in a suburb may come in with a detailed draft contract school board members find hard to believe. The local shopkeeper who serves on the unpaid board out of civic duty usually cannot take the time to sit down and think about counterproposals. Bargaining becomes a one-way street with demands by the teachers' group and a fall-back response by the board.

On the school board's side, the management team has divided loyalties. Even the superintendents were once teachers themselves, and until quite recently they were members of the teachers' association now threatening to strike. On the middle-management level, each principal wishes to avoid being placed in conflict situations in opposition to the teachers with whom he must work in intimate professional collaboration.

The prospect of a strike is an emotional powder keg, and the board fears that failure to make a deal may do permanent damage to the team spirit and morale of the district's schools. And the public has no interest in "details." School board members get little or no credit for fighting "the good fight," battling through long and weary sessions to preserve those important intangibles. In fact, the school board that fights to preserve public control of the schools may find itself publicly condemned for nit picking and intransigence.

What the public will not stand for, in many cities, is the imposition of new taxes. In the private sector, unions often agree to moderate their wage demands after full disclosure of the economic health of the industry because they recognize that going beyond a certain point will bankrupt the enterprise. That kind of economic discipline does not seem to exist in public sector collective bargaining. When a union does recognize that the local board has no way of raising additional revenue, the results may be even more devastating to the public interest.

A board that can no longer bargain on salaries because there is no money begins to make concessions on the governance of the schools.

Some negotiated contracts with school boards already give teachers the right to bargain on questions of the curriculum, class size, selection of personnel, promotion, transfer, selection of textbooks, and just about everything that goes on in the school. The Task Force ran into one case where a principal was required to seek faculty senate approval before he could call a fire drill, even though monthly fire drills were mandated by state statute.

Personnel Practices

A major battleground in today's school bargainings is the question of accountability. There is a great deal of concern in the profession and among the public about the issue of who should be accountable for what. The battle to make school personnel accountable for the outcome of their work can be lost in the negotiating room and the public will never get a chance to say anything about it. Even the established procedures of program evaluation—including the evaluation of teachers and administrators—are being eroded at the bargaining table. When a parent complains about a teacher, it seems to the parent that he or she is placed on the defensive since the teacher has all of the "due process" rights, including representation by the union's lawyer. The public comes to be seen as a trouble-making nuisance in the public school.

Many recently negotiated contracts require the exclusive use of certified people in the schools. Teacher organizations contend that everyone who works with children must hold teaching certificates. Community people cannot be used in school programs and school buildings cannot be opened for greater community participation when the district has a written contract imposing the requirement that every important duty in the school be performed by a certified person.

Teachers are, of course, perfectly willing to have uncertified people do the less rewarding jobs—indeed, many contracts now require that lesser-skilled personnel be hired to perform auxiliary tasks. Teachers now expect the school board to employ security personnel to monitor the halls and restrooms and handle discipline problems, and many contracts relieve teachers of all responsibility for supervising play areas and lunchrooms.

Moreover, the teacher organizations have begun to extend their use of muscle from the bargaining table to the political arena. Helen Wise, president of the National Education Association, called a press conference in the spring of 1974 to announce that the NEA plans to raise $5 million to $6 million to elect a new Congress that "cares about education." "We got our political feet wet in 1972," says Dr. Wise. "We learned the process well; our skills are sharpened now, and we will work for our goals across the nation. . . . It is our intent to translate our successes in the congressional elections of 1974 into a mandate to elect a friend of education to the White House in 1976."

These self-aggrandizements have not gone unopposed. Taxpayers are digging in their heels: every year, school systems lose more and more millage campaigns. Opposing groups contend that the additional millage would be used to pay for the teachers' contract and not to pay for improvements in the educational program. Nearly 80 percent of the school budget in many cities is now controlled by the teachers' contract.

In the early days of collective bargaining, there was little public resistance to teacher organization. Most citizens were sympathetic with the need for teacher salaries to catch up on lost ground. As the teacher organizations begin to push over into the educational side, however, citizen resistance will increase. Civic groups are raising serious questions about the quality and effect of citizen involvement in today's school systems. Even more disquieting is the emergence of the attitude that "these are not our schools, but rather something that is being captured and run by somebody else."

Principals and Collective Bargaining

With the success of the teacher organizations has come a movement to organize school principals. Principals have always been considered management personnel and, under many state laws and classic labor-management law, employees with management responsibilities are excluded from collective-bargaining rights. To organize, principals must maintain that they are not a part of management and will not participate in the management process.

Some principals who take this position refuse to advise school boards about the implications of teachers' contract demands and refuse to participate in any meaningful way in the administration of the teachers' contract. In New York City, they have made this position effective: following a series of hearings, the state's Public Employment Relations Board (PERB) ruled that New York City school principals are not managerial personnel. The board concluded that principals (1) do not have a major role to play in the development of school policy, (2) cannot reasonably be required to participate in preparations for collective bargaining with teachers, (3) have no significant role to play in the administration of a teacher contract, and (4) have no important function in personnel administration. The Public Education Association of New York City was dismayed by this decision, so community involvement groups have initiated an appeal and the final decision is before the courts. Their position is that if principals are not part of management the schools do not need principals at all.[1]

Obviously, a principals' union can be effective only if teachers will honor its picket lines. A principals' organization, however separate it may proclaim itself to be, must ultimately become an adjunct of the teachers' organization. Top management in education must move immediately to improve the status of school principals, or risk losing the allegiance of the cadre most observers consider the key to quality education. As part of the improvement in the status of principals, school systems must abandon the common compensation patterns that tie the principals' salary schedule to a ratio such as 1.73 times the base teacher salary. A school board cannot realistically say that the principal is part of management when he benefits directly by a multiplier of whatever increase the teachers' union can win for its members. No doubt the first result of such a change will be a larger increase in principals' salaries, but by assuring the loyalty of principals to management roles the revision will be cheap at the price.

NOTE

1. Excerpt of remarks made by David S. Seeley, director, Public Education Association, New York City, to members of Task Force '74 at a meeting in Portland, Oregon, on May 20, 1974.

PART III

STUDENT RESPONSIBILITIES

CHAPTER 5

Identifying Student Responsibilities

"They [the students] are possessed of fundamental rights which the State must respect, just as they themselves must respect their obligations to the State. . . ."[1]

Recommendation No. 11

The Task Force realizes that schools will not improve significantly unless individual student rights are balanced with individual student responsibilities to the school and society. Therefore, it is recommended that each high school further the opportunity for citizen involvement by establishing a committee composed of students, teachers, administrators, and community representatives broadly chosen for the purpose of identifying, posting, and widely disseminating in the school's literature the responsibilities students are expected to accept.

The National Commission on the Reform of Secondary Education commented with dismay in 1973 at the lack of concern displayed in the high schools for student responsibility to the school community and the larger society. Having reviewed a wide sampling of school publications dealing with the topic of student rights and responsibilities, the Commissioners expressed alarm that "about 99 percent of the content of these documents deals with student rights and less than 1 percent with responsibilities."

Recent emphasis by the courts on student rights highlights the need for attention by the schools to student responsibilities. Research on this subject is nil, and the literature generally is very thin. Schools are operating in almost complete ignorance of the responsibilities of their clientele—and students, inevitably, know less than their schools.

Rights v. Responsibilities

Neither "rights" nor "responsibilities" is an easy word to define. Rights are a legal requirement; for the violation of rights, the law provides remedies. Responsibilities, on the other hand, are not so clearly spelled out. Rights are stated; responsibilities are tacit. "Rights" adhere to the individual; "responsibilities" involve relations with others.

Rights, as John Stuart Mill emphasized a century ago, must terminate at that point where they begin to impinge upon the rights of others. To the extent that responsibilities are fulfilled, rights become more assured. To the extent responsibilities are not met, rights are placed in jeopardy.

For the purpose of this report, responsibilities are defined as the foundation upon which individual rights become meaningful and effective.

Criteria for School Rules

According to E. Edmund Reutter, students can be held responsible for rules that meet the following standards:

• The rules must be known to students (not necessarily written). If the act for which the student is to be punished is obviously destructive or disruptive, no rule is necessary.

• The rules must have a proper educational purpose connected to learning itself. (When schools enforce rules relating to societal norms of hair styles, lengths of skirts or other clothing standards, problems arise.)

• The rules must be reasonably clear in meaning. (The statement "Students may not wear provocative symbols" is unacceptable to the courts because "provocative" is not defined.)

• The rules must be narrow to avoid trespassing on some protected right. (If a rule states that literature shall be distributed only before school, at noon, and after school, the rule is constitutionally sound. If the rule forbids distribution of literature produced off campus, it is unconstitutional.)[2]

Student Responsibilities

The most extensive analysis of student responsibilities was developed by the State Department of Education in Michigan.[3] Creation of the Michigan guidelines involved students, parents, teachers, and school administrators. The Task Force acknowledges its indebtedness to this document in preparing the following list of eleven student responsibilities that should be assumed as a balance to student rights:

1. Each student has a responsibility to observe the constitutional rights of other individuals, whether they are students,

parents, teachers, school officials, or other participants in the educational process.

Knowledge of constitutional rights for all must be stressed in school programs.

2. Each student has the responsibility to respect the inherent human dignity and worth of every other individual.

When a student disrupts a class, making it difficult or impossible for other students to fulfill their function as learning members of that class, he is expressing a disrespect for their dignity.

3. Each student has the responsibility to be informed of, and adhere to, reasonable rules and regulations established by the board of education and implemented by school administrators and teachers for the welfare and safety of all students.

Student responsibility to obey regulations restricts student rights—but ultimately that restriction becomes the students' best assurance of the acknowledgment of all rights. If, for example, school-initiated discipline codes are based largely on the need to carry forward the educational process, students and their parents will know that everyone's right to an education in nondisruptive surroundings is assured.

4. Each student should assume the responsibility for recognition of individual and cultural differences and knowledge as to how to use those differences for the improvement of society.

Students must recognize and accept the reality that American schools and society are pluralistic, composed of individuals of heterogeneous national origins and varied customs and beliefs. All citizens must be afforded human rights, including the right to participation.

Students must be guided toward a willingness to interact with individuals and groups different from themselves. They should learn that recognition of differences is a means of preserving individuality while building group loyalty.

5. Each student has the responsibility to dress and appear in a manner that meets reasonable standards of health, cleanliness, and safety.

School districts should attempt to regulate dress and grooming of students only to the extent that violations of the rules would disrupt the learning process or present a health or safety hazard. The choice of dress is the student's and not the school's so long as he does not dress in a manner which violates reasonable standards of cleanliness, health, and safety.

6. Each student has a responsibility for the development of employment skills relevant to economic independence throughout his or her life span.

In acquiring the work orientation which is essential for successful employment, students must develop during high school those skills of communication and computation that are important for functioning productively.

High school students must also have opportunities to develop a variety of general skills that contribute to the performance of various kinds of employment, including persistence, resistance to distraction, perseverance upon encountering obstacles, and the ability to see tasks through to completion.

7. Each student has a responsibility for maintaining the best possible level of academic achievement.

This implies diligent study which, in itself, is education for responsibility.

8. Each student has a responsibility to refrain from libel, slanderous remarks, and obscenity in verbal and written expression, and all students engaged in school media programs should state explicitly on all media produced that the opinions expressed are not necessarily those of the institution or of the student body as a whole.

This applies not only to classroom decorum, but also to extracurricular behavior. Among the areas of immediate concern are school newspapers, literary journals, and other student-oriented publications produced by high school students. In recent years, this sphere of school activities has become one of increased concern to school officials as students have questioned the appropriateness of school control in what students tend to consider "their" publications. In addition, the so-called "underground" newspapers have drawn increased attention.

9. **Each student must develop and undertake a social commitment if he or she is to assume some responsibility to and for school and society.**

This is an important responsibility because it calls for positive action, not just the avoidance of negative behavior. It is one thing for a student not to be destructive, but quite another for that student to make a commitment to show others the value of not being destructive.

10. **Each student must assume responsibility to observe, know, and adhere to the laws of the state in which he or she resides.**

If this responsibility were recognized by all students, it would dispel what has been called by school officials "the largest single discipline problem faced by public schools in the nation"—smoking in the schools. Most states have laws specifying that no person under the age of eighteen may purchase or possess cigarettes. In schools which permit student smoking "lounges" similar to the facilities maintained for teachers, student lounges must be used only by students eighteen or older. On the other hand, a school that absolutely forbids student smoking while allowing teachers to smoke in their own lounge may run into legal problems if the state has an age of majority law concerning eighteen-year-olds. Allowing adult teachers to smoke at school but refusing adult students the same privilege is viewed by some constitutional attorneys as an abridgement of the Fourteenth Amendment rights.

11. Each student has the responsibility to preserve school property, exercise care while using school facilities, and help maintain and improve the school environment consistent with laws governing such property.

The national concern for ecology must be brought down to an individual, personal level for each student in relation to his school environment. Adolescent litter is in no way better than adult litter, and school property is protected by the same laws that protect the student's own property. If high school students are to develop responsibility to and for schools and society in relation to laws and regulations, they must receive effective instruction and practical experiences in the American system of justice.

NOTES

1. *Tinker v. Des Moines Independent Community School District,* 393 U.S. 503 (1969).

2. Remarks made by E. Edmund Reutter, Jr., professor of education, Columbia University (N.Y.), Teachers College, to members of Task Force '74 at a meeting in Atlanta, Georgia, on March 12, 1974.

3. Michigan Department of Education, *Recommended Guidelines for Students' Rights and Responsibilities in Michigan,* April 30, 1974.

CHAPTER 6

Educating for Responsibility Through the High School Curriculum

Recommendation No. 12

The Task Force believes that a sense of these responsibilities is best acquired when students have the opportunity to assume responsibility as a way of learning the relationship between actions and consequences. An interdisciplinary approach is suggested which will place particular emphasis on the areas of English and social studies. Therefore, it is recommended that substantial state and federal resources be allocated for research and development designed to implement a new focus on student responsibilities, utilizing an interdisciplinary curricular approach.

High schools have become virtually the only institutional setting in which adolescents are socialized to an adult world.

They have gained this position by default in a society which does not need and does not want adolescents in the job market. Among the consequences has been the growth of a peer culture in large part isolated from the rest of society. Young persons now spend most of their time in schools in almost total isolation from adults, except for school personnel. The only social role available to them is that of student.

Some high schools as presently organized are not suitable environments for adolescents learning to become responsible adults. Primarily oriented toward cognitive achievement, these schools impose dependency on and withhold responsibility from students. They have evolved in this manner not by design, but by failure to make adjustments in organization and programs to accommodate the expanded purposes of education.

The holy alliance of school skills has been "readin', 'ritin', and 'rithmetic." To the three R's, a fourth R—responsibility—must be added. The focus of this study must be the balance between individual rights and social responsibility; and the program should be instituted immediately.

The conventional technique for educating about responsibility employs a scattering of courses in civics and American history and is clearly inadequate. By far the most interesting effort now in sight is the new program of the American Bar Association (ABA) through its Special Committee on Youth Education for Citizenship. The materials published by this group are exciting. The Task Force hopes the ABA will persist in balancing the responsibilities with the rights of citizenship.[1]

The Development of Moral and Ethical Values

Learning about responsibility is very much a part of moral education. Professor Lawrence Kohlberg has identified six stages of moral development.

In the most primitive stage, perceptions of good and bad are governed by the prospect of reward and punishment and the power of those making the rules. By stage four, the individual obeys rules out of respect for authority and the social order. At the highest stage, principles of justice determine the individual's decisions. According to Kohlberg's theory, the development of moral reasoning is sequential, and growth may cease here as in the development of skills before the individual reaches advanced stages. Kohlberg concludes that education can accelerate or retard the processes of moral development.

Kohlberg's six stages of moral growth form a blueprint for the construction of moral education curricula. These are:

1. Orientation to punishment and reward and to physical and material power
2. Beginning notions of reciprocity but with emphasis on exchange—"You scratch my back and I'll scratch yours"
3. "Good Boy" orientation—seeking to maintain expectations and win approval of one's immediate group
4. Orientation to authority, law, and duty
5. An emphasis on the protection of individual rights by a democratic established order
6. Morality of self-chosen principles which, while self-chosen, are universalized to all men[2]

In all discussions of teaching of moral values, questions are raised about the right of teachers to impose values on adolescents. But any group that is committed to the notion of rights for students cannot escape the development of a sense of justice as a desideratum in moral education. Kohlberg's approach to moral education involves the student's own development of moral principles rather than the indoctrination of conventional opinion.

An Action Program

Over thirty years ago, James Bryant Conant wrote of the need for an emphasis on educating for responsibility:

The primary concern of American education today is not the development of the appreciation of the "good life" in young gentlemen born to the purple. . . . Our purpose is to cultivate in the largest possible number of our future citizens an appreciation of both the responsibilities and the benefits which come to them because they are Americans and are free.[3]

The strategy for achieving this reform must be interdisciplinary, but for this purpose the disciplines are not equally valuable. Social studies, English, and literature are clearly relevant to moral and ethical education in ways that mathematics and physical science are not. But the traditional civics approach to teaching citizenship has not been effective. The casual visit to the local courthouse, for example, has not been a legitimate field experience. Teaching young people about responsibility and citizenship requires that they be sent out into the community to acquire experience in our system of civil and criminal justice at work. As part of their training in citizenship, students should spend part of each day of this project period working in the courts, in judges' chambers, in probation offices, in police headquarters, in law offices.

The goal of such a program is to enable young people to cope with conflicts of values—not just conflicts between good and bad, but confrontations among rules and attitudes all perceived as good.

Substantial resources must be allocated to the development of curricula containing significant components of moral and ethical values. These programs require the active participation of educators, legal scholars, and a broad mix of citizens.

Educating for Responsibility

Active and effective citizenship grows from participatory involvement in decision making and decision monitoring. This growth can be stimulated by an educational atmosphere conducive to the understanding of freedom, the interplay of ideas and self-expression, and the trial-error process of developing ever-broadening responsibilities.

The Task Force's concept of educating for responsibility stresses student responsibility to and for school and society. The following are the most important elements:

Employment is central to education for responsibility. Adolescents who have received necessary life-supporting resources simply because they are themselves must learn that as adults they will have to perform tasks that society expects of all of its citizens. Most students do look forward, for various reasons and with varying degrees of enthusiasm, to productive futures. But they do not necessarily understand the relationships between the skills acquired in school and future employability. Both general and specific skills related to employment can best be developed through extensive programs in career education.

A knowledge of major life roles is essential in educating for responsibility because adolescents must become aware of obligations inherent in all adult interpersonal relationships. To understand role performance, students must have opportunities to discharge a variety of life roles themselves and to interact with others in a variety of situations.

The obligations entailed by various roles may at times be incompatible. Students must learn to tolerate ambiguities, to resolve conflicts, and to apportion their resources of time and energy among their role commitments. A knowledge of roles is necessary for adequate functioning within the school as well as in the larger society.

Social commitment must be developed for the student to assume responsibility to school and society. Social commitment relates to the present and future welfare of the school and society. It involves feelings of community with others and willingness to modify or relinquish personal goals to advance community goals.

During the high school years, social commitment begins as identification with various groups: family, classmates, the student body, neighbors, community, state, nation, and the world. High schools, then, must provide varied opportunities for association and interaction among students. Individuals show their major group identifications by their assignment of priorities among competing goals.

Important goals are seldom achieved by the actions of individuals alone. Therefore, high school students must be made aware of the need to make alliances and compromises with others. Students must learn that some problems do not lend themselves to immediate solutions and that the ability to work over sustained periods of time must be cultivated.

Ethical standards. Both the ends and the means of social commitment will be profoundly influenced by the ethical standards of the individual participants. Part of instruction in responsibility must be the teaching of values clarification which rejects the sacrifice of moral judgment for an allegedly "higher" goal.

For adolescents, questions of responsibility and ethical standards arise most often in the context of sexuality. Sex education is an inescapable requirement for the modern high school.

Recognition and appreciation of individual and cultural differences must also be a component of educating for responsibility, as noted on page 48.

Law. An important end of educating for responsibility is the promotion of a new "civism" appropriate to the principles of a just society in the United States and a just world community. The general guidelines of a new civism can be found in the principles of justice, liberty, and equality, summarized in the Constitution and the Bill of Rights. As one of the original signers of the Constitution wrote, "Law and liberty cannot rationally become the objects of our love unless they first become the objects of our knowledge." [4] High school courses in American law, however, must not be focused solely on abstract Constitutional questions, or on community standards, but also on the day-to-day functioning of the rule of law.

Politics. Students must be taught to deal effectively with the political system and to understand that in a democracy political participation involves the acceptance of defeat as well as the fruits of victory. They must also realize that changes in the political system which seek to correct injustice may create an initial period of disequilibrium but will eventually lead to a more firm and satisfying equilibrium.

Since many high school students will have attained the age of majority before graduation, acquisition of political understanding during high school is necessary. In addition to political science courses, experiences as members of youth clubs of various political parties and direct participation in political campaigns present worthwhile opportunities for growth in understanding.

Changes in the School Environment

To educate for responsibility, educators must change the organizational structure of the schools and the content of their instruction. Substantial state and federal resources should be allocated for research and development to make these changes.

ORGANIZATIONAL STRUCTURE

Schools organized along authoritarian lines are unable to foster environments conducive to individual development. In an atmosphere of coercion and regimentation, students cannot be asked to display responsible behavior derived from interaction with their environment, so they live up to expectations and passively pursue the route through school. Then they are expected to emerge from these isolated educational institutions as productive and enlightened citizens, never having experienced opportunities to exercise the responsibilities of citizenship. In regard to organizational structure, this study concludes:

• High schools must become functional models of just societies in which all individuals affected by decisions have an inherent right to participate in reaching those decisions.

• High schools must provide organizational plans that allow for daring and imaginative use of resources including time, space, funds, and personnel.

• High schools must capitalize on what teachers do best and are most knowledgeable about by rearranging staffing patterns as necessary. Working in conjunction, faculty and staff members can exploit their own strengths and receive help for their weaknesses.

• High schools must make the transition from a form of bureaucratic paternalism to institutions fostering increased community participation. This implies the need for established channels through which parents and citizens at large can participate effectively in the educational process.

• High schools must seek to eliminate adversary relationships between instructional personnel and students and foster collaborative efforts.

THE CURRICULUM AND CHANGING VALUES

The Task Force believes that a chief priority of curriculum planning should be to develop curricula that will strengthen a sense of responsibility, social cohesion, and commitment to citizenship on the part of the nation's young people. *Indeed, the most needed reform in American education*

is a new and more viable emphasis on the responsibilities of
citizenship from kindergarten to high school.

The Task Force's position on the critical need for a new and
greater emphasis on citizenship education is supported by the
National Assessment of Educational Progress which reported
last year that students had little knowledge about the responsibilities of effective citizenship and its appropriate processes.

The recent report of the Yankelovich study of youth's values
in the seventies tends to support the National Assessment results in that it documents significant shifts in the attitudes of
America's youth toward long-held traditional values. The Yankelovich report compared the values of young Americans between the ages of sixteen and twenty-five with those who were
in the same group in the late sixties. The survey revealed that
significant large-scale changes have occurred in the social values of adolescents within the last six years. The changes are so
abrupt, Yankelovich concluded that they mark the end of one
era of values held by American youth and the beginning of another. Among the "New Values" which Yankelovich reported
were:

(1) changes in sexual morality in the direction of more
liberal sexual mores;

(2) changes in relation to the authority of institutions
such as the authority of law, the police, the government,
the boss in the work situation, etc.; the changes here are in
the direction of what sociologists call "deauthorization,"
i.e., a lessening of automatic obedience to, and respect for,
established authority;

(3) changes in views toward the church and organized
religion as a source of guidance for moral behavior; and

(4) changes in traditional concepts of patriotism and in
automatic allegiance to "my country right or wrong."

The second category of New Values relates to social
values, primarily to changing attitudes toward the work

ethic, marriage and family, and the role and importance of money in defining the meaning of success.

The third category of New Values concerns the meaning of the vague concept of self-fulfillment. Self-fulfillment is usually defined by people today in opposition to the concern with economic security. Once a person feels that he can take some degree of economic security for granted, he begins to look forward to relief from the discipline of a constant preoccupation with economic security, and he starts to search for forms of self-fulfillment that go beyond the daily routine. Stress on the theme of gratification is the individual's way of saying that there must be something more to life than making a living, struggling to make ends meet, and caring for others. The self-fulfillment concept also implies a greater preoccupation with self at the expense of sacrificing one's self for family, employer and community.[5]

The most striking finding of this study and the one which could result in the most impact upon the high school is the extent to which the differences in values between college preparatory and noncollege preparatory youth has blended over the past six years. Noncollege youth who have been traditionally more conservative seem to be arriving at value orientations much akin to those of their more liberal college-bound peers.

The results of the Yankelovich Study seem to corroborate two significant trends. First, it seems today's youth have less of an appreciation of the functions of "citizenship." Second, it seems that the values on which "citizenship" are based have undergone serious changes within the last six years. These changes make it incumbent upon the high school to undertake a concerted effort in whatever part of the school's curriculum and program is necessary to cope with these two issues.

The challenge to the schools is to no longer attempt to avoid the clash of ideas and value systems which resound in society but to meet them head on through curricular revision. The use of the term values in the curricular sense means that set of attitudes, beliefs, commitments, and obligations that contribute to functioning in a democratic society. This very much needs to be part of today's secondary school program.

NOTES

1. Special Committee on Youth Education for Citizenship, *Help! What to Do, Where to Go?* (Chicago, Ill.: American Bar Association, 1973).

2. Remarks made by Professor Lawrence Kohlberg, Harvard Graduate School of Education, at a meeting of Task Force '74, in Boston, Massachusetts, Apr. 8, 1974.

3. James B. Conant, *Annual Report to the Board of Overseers,* Harvard University, Boston, Mass., Jan. 11, 1943.

4. James Wilson, justice of the United States Supreme Court and signer of the Declaration of Independence and the Constitution.

5. Daniel Yankelovich, *Changing Youth Values in the 70's: A Study of American Youth,* jointly sponsored by Edna McConnell Clark Foundation, Carnegie Corporation of New York, Hazen Foundation, JDR 3rd Fund, and Andrew W. Mellon Foundation, 1973.

PART IV

ALTERNATIVE PROGRAMS AS EDUCATIONAL OPTIONS WITHIN THE FRAMEWORK OF THE LOCAL SCHOOL DISTRICT

CHAPTER 7

Alternative Programs as Educational Options

Recommendation No. 13

The Task Force believes that the community college is a viable alternative to the last year of high school for many students. Therefore, it is recommended that action be taken by state departments of education to facilitate and coordinate the movement of high school students into the community colleges and to eliminate the "battle for bodies" now being waged between high school and community college personnel.

Recommendation No. 14

The Task Force urges school districts to move toward a systemwide range of alternatives responsive to the needs of all students. Therefore, it is recommended that school boards and superintendents take steps to coordinate the efforts of principals, teachers, citizens, and students in the development of alternative programs so that the fragmentation of current efforts may be replaced by systemwide planning.

American high schools perform reasonably well in providing educational programs that meet the needs of the majority of students. There is much in the public high schools that should be retained. But many students are not well served by the comprehensive high school and require alternative programs. *Task Force '74 defines the term "alternative programs" to mean optional programs which help to complete the educational role of the high school regardless of size of student population or the location of the enterprise.* These alternative programs, once implemented, become new ways in which students can succeed in the high school experience. This part of the report deals with the reasons for providing such alternatives, with recommended strategies, and with roadblocks that may have to be removed as new programs are implemented. It also provides a model timeline for the development of alternative programs and suggestions of elements that must be addressed in the move from conception to implementation.

Alternatives Outside the Traditional High Schools

Pressure for new educational options has been building for many years. "Free" schools have sprung up outside the public schools; flexible-modular scheduling has been employed to reduce the rigidity of traditional course offerings; and a number of school systems are presently operating alternative programs, "magnet" schools, and skills centers. The popularity of these reforms indicates a consumer demand which should provide sufficient incentive for a major restructuring of high school education.

"FREE" SCHOOLS

"Free" schools offer an uninhibited open environment in which students may or may not learn. Students are encouraged to establish their own classes and learning environments. In addition to academic studies, "free" schools focus on flexibility and the student's development of self-reliance, decision-making ability, and responsibility.

PUBLIC ALTERNATIVE SCHOOLS OR "MAGNET" SCHOOLS

Many public school districts operate specialized high schools available to all students within the district. Students who seek enriched learning opportunities in this school's area of specialization apply for admission. An area of specialization might be any one of the broad curricular divisions or a specific career cluster such as art and design, performing and visual arts, or the health professions. Many of these schools offer complete interdisciplinary programs which attempt to correlate all required courses with the particular specialty. The curricula usually are structured so that students may develop entry-level skills in their specialities or skills and knowledge sufficient to increase their likelihood of success in further training at the post-secondary level.

SKILLS CENTERS

A skills center customarily concentrates resources for service to students from all the high schools in a given area or district. Career-oriented students may spend a portion of the day attending academic classes in regular high schools and the remaining hours in centers for development of specific job skills. Transportation is usually provided.

COMMUNITY COLLEGES AS AN ALTERNATIVE FOR HIGH SCHOOL STUDENTS

Community colleges must be viewed as viable alternatives for high school students. The tremendous expansion of the community college movement, coupled with state school codes that permit the enrollment of high school students in such institutions, gives this alternative national significance.

In California, which is leading the movement, the president of any two-year community college may admit to the college, on a part-time basis, eleventh- or twelfth-grade students who are recommended by their principals. The principal may recommend as many as 15 percent of the eleventh- and twelfth-grade students enrolled in his school.

Oregon and Washington are also moving rapidly toward breaking the barrier between high schools and community colleges. In Washington in 1973, the legislature amended the Community College Act to permit fifteen-year-olds who have completed ninth grade with good marks to enroll in community colleges. In Oregon, high school students can receive a high school diploma using community college credit.

The community college is an excellent alternative for many students, and many will wish to use it. A student who takes a course in calculus at the high school level must put in a minimum of 120 hours—usually 180—before getting credit. He can complete the same course in the community college in 48 hours.

Unfortunately, this alternative creates a tug-of-war for students between the community college president and the high school principal. The high school principal is reluctant to release his better students, and the community college president wants them badly to increase his enrollment—and to increase the highly able fraction of his student body.

The competition is becoming so keen that within the next five years the high schools could lose the twelfth grade entirely. With the decline in college enrollments, the colleges are lowering their standards for admission and aggressively recruiting high school students before graduation.

And four-year colleges are beginning to enter the competition. The Union for Experimenting Colleges and Universities recently reported that it has begun High School-College/Universities Without Walls in six states to admit high school juniors as college students and implement integrated programs that will yield a high school diploma en route to the college degree. The Union refers to this effort as "not merely an early admission program, but a concerted attempt . . . to break the artificial barriers which are tied to the coincidence of chronological age."[1]

Alternatives Within Traditional High Schools

The remainder of this chapter focuses on the establishment of educational alternatives within existing high schools as a means of effectively confronting the needs and interests of the entire student population. The rationale for providing alternative programs in existing schools are (1) educational desirability, (2) financial feasibility, and (3) public acceptability. These reasons are discussed below:

EDUCATIONAL DESIRABILITY

Alternative programs are educationally desirable because they offer significant choices for parents, students, and teachers among a variety of approaches to teaching and learning. The provision of alternatives does not alter the established functions of schools but rather the methods and processes through which these functions are performed. Students can engage in significant decision making as they choose among options and activities. Even in required courses, individual variations should be allowed by encouraging student participation in identifying and suggesting appropriate learning activities.

One universal criticism of the high school relates to its failure to motivate the "dropout" and the "sit-in." Task Force '74 believes this criticism is justified. Its members doubt, however, whether significant progress in reaching the unmotivated student can be realized within traditional structures. Alternative programs enable students to contract for a content and style of learning which meets their individual needs. Increased motivation should result from individualized instruction. It is time for school personnel to cease expecting students to match programs and to start providing programs that match students. However, criteria for excellence should always be maintained so that an alternative does not become a dumping ground.

FINANCIAL FEASIBILITY

The establishment of alternative programs in existing schools is financially feasible. In most instances, existing per-pupil budgets will cover basic costs. As noted in the following pages, additional funds may be needed for minor alteration of buildings, for surveys and planning, and for other start-up costs; but these increases can conceivably be offset by savings realized from the elimination of continuation or high school equivalency programs, and remedial courses. Alternative programs should decrease the need for such stop-gap measures.

PUBLIC ACCEPTABILITY

Public acceptance of alternative programs in schools is increasing. The *Fifth Annual Survey of the Public's Attitudes Toward the Public Schools* indicated that 62 percent of the parents of public school students and 80 percent of the professional educators believe the establishment of such programs to be a good idea.[2]

Characteristics of Successful Alternative Programs Within Traditional High Schools

GOAL ORIENTATION

Successful alternative programs are usually consistent with the general goals of high school education. But their statements of objectives should be quite comprehensive and specialized, and an ongoing evaluation process must be established. While these programs seek the development of basic skills and career preparation, they are also concerned with the improvement of self-concepts, the development of individual talent, the understanding and encouragement of plurality and diversity, and the preparation of students for various roles in society—consumer, producer, voter, critic, spouse, parent.

INDIVIDUAL ORIENTATION

A variety of significant choices are available to individual students in an alternative setting, and students are permitted to change options without penalty. As a result, the selection of a particular program does not foreclose other options. The curricula should be relevant to the interests, needs, abilities, and life and learning styles of the students who choose them. The primary focus is on individuality rather than conformity.

FLEXIBILITY

Good alternative programs are customarily quite flexible in time and place arrangements so that students are not locked into daily time sequences. Instead, flexibility in scheduling allows the allocation of time to be related to the program the students are pursuing. The learning environment may be far removed from the classroom and may be chosen by the students in consultation with teachers who become facilitators or managers of learning.

SMALL ENROLLMENTS

In the alternative frame, the high school student body is divided into sub-enrollments within individual programs. This provides opportunities for meaningful interaction between students and teachers. It is an antidote to the dehumanization process which is inherent in any large, bureaucratic institution.

Small enrollments generally result in fewer rules and administrative constraints for teachers and students. Consequently, students are more accepted as full partners in the process of education.

FLEXIBLE GRADING

Grading practices are flexible and offer a variety of different measurements among which students and parents can choose.

FLEXIBLE CREDENTIALING

The structure for awarding credits is a function of the program the student chooses. Methods include credit by examination, completion of objectives, demonstrated competency, and completion of contractual agreements.

Alternative Program Structure and Curricular Variations Within the Traditional High Schools

Variations within the high school can be categorized under two broad headings: (1) degree of structure, including space utilization and time allocations and (2) curricular design and students served. The variations possible in alternative programs are discussed below under appropriate headings.

STRUCTURE

• *Nonstructured.* Programs are community-linked and experience-based. All learning experiences are selected by students; parents and teachers provide resource materials and advise students who explore their own interests. There are no scheduled instructional meetings; teachers are available as advisers when needed. The entire community is the learning environment.

• *Open Structure.* Students have considerable freedom to choose from a wide range of content areas considered relevant by themselves, parents, and teachers. Students and their advisers together identify experiences and activities which will be undertaken. These are not restricted to the classroom, but exploit community-based learning opportunities. Resource centers in major skill areas may be provided at centralized locations. Teachers serve as supportive facilitators of learning in student-centered programs.

• *Modified Structure.* Content is prescribed but is made flexible through individualization of instruction. Programs are ungraded; different students learn the same things but at different rates. Teachers may utilize team teaching and are encouraged to plan differentiated approaches to instruction which normally take place in the school building. Some teacher-student planning occurs, but programs are largely teacher directed.

• *Standardized Structure.* Students adhere to institutional requirements which prescribe what is to be taught—how, where, when, and with whom. They move from grade to grade on a yearly basis providing minimum academic standards are met. Teachers are responsible for outcomes as defined in the curriculum and students pass or fail according to normative standards. Assigned classrooms and study areas within the building comprise the learning environment.

• *Flexible-Modular Scheduling Structure.* In schools employing modular scheduling, students generally have 30 to 50 percent of their time unscheduled. The unscheduled time is utilized in independent-study-type activities, open labs and, in many instances, community-based learning activities. However, *conventionally designed schools may have insufficient resources to challenge students who are given extensive blocks of unscheduled time.*

CURRICULAR DESIGN AND UNIQUE OPTIONS

A variety of curricular designs can be offered through program modifications which permit students to choose academic programs that most nearly approximate their needs, interests, and learning styles. Several designs are discussed as follows:

• *Independent Study Curriculum.* Curriculum is completely designed by individual students who also develop goals, select content and activities, and evaluate progress. Students assume total responsibility for learning with counseling available as needed through a faculty adviser or team of advisers. Traditionally, independent study has been restricted to exceptional students; but all students should have this option available.

• *Basic Skills.* Curriculum is designed to strengthen basic skills as a means of improving achievement. All courses are geared to basic skills development. These programs are chosen by students who recognize weaknesses in skills areas and are seeking to improve their capabilities.

• *Arts and Humanities.* Curriculum is organized around a core in the areas of visual and performing arts, literature, language arts, and history. All course work is correlated to the particular core area. Students usually have special aptitude for the chosen area and expect to develop entry-level skills or knowledge and skills necessary for post-secondary training.

• *Technology and Careers.* Curriculum is organized around specific technological areas or career clusters. All instruction relates to the career cluster or area of technology. Students expect to graduate with entry-level skills or knowledge and skills necessary for post-secondary training.

• *Multi-Cultural.* Curriculum is designed to emphasize cultural pluralism. All courses are taught from a multi-cultural perspective and include cultural exchange and joint classes. Programs are customarily chosen by students who are interested in improving their understanding of their own culture and the many cultures represented in today's pluralistic society.

• *Dropout Prevention.* Curriculum is organized around content and processes designed to show the connections between education and life experiences. Extensive counseling is an integral part of the program and some out-of-school work is included. Students in this program have experienced little or no success in standardized programs and, consequently, no positive reinforcement of their efforts. The probability of their dropping out is decreased through "zero reject" instructional techniques.

Current Approaches to the Establishment of Alternatives both Within and Without the Traditional High School

INITIATIVE OF ADMINISTRATORS AND TEACHERS

Initiative for the creation of alternatives may come from an innovative administrator who has to sell the idea to his teachers and the central office—or from groups of interested teachers who may find it difficult to convince administrators that their idea has merit. Optimum conditions for successful innovation grow from a joint initiative of administrators and teachers. Unfortunately, proposals from within the school are usually designed for specific target groups and serve limited fractions of the student population. Students often seek entry because a particular program may be the only alternative to the traditional program rather than because it is best suited to their needs, interests, and life and learning styles.

INFLUENCE OF PARENTS AND CITIZENS

Groups of influential and affluent parents who were dissatisfied with public education pooled their resources and skills to establish "free" schools in the 1960s. Very few of these schools have survived; meanwhile, this leadership cadre has not used its influence to promote changes within the public high school. Often the reason for their disaffection has been opposition from school boards. When their initiatives are successful, the resulting programs usually focus on a single target group rather than serving a significant number of the student body.

STUDENT ACTIVISM

Increasing numbers of high school students are disenchanted with the current educational system. Instead of dropping out, they seek to effect changes from within. In many instances these students are high achievers and would succeed under any system, but a desire to become personally involved in the educational process spurs them to action. These student groups usually cooperate with teachers who are sympathetic to their cause and support proposals presented to school administrators. If the administration accepts a proposal, the supportive teachers frequently become the staff. As in the previous situations, only the interests of a small group are normally served.

Acting as separate forces, administrators, teachers, citizens, and students usually initiate only a piecemeal reform in which alternative programs are made available to only a limited number of students. Even though the programs have some impact, the fact that they are fragmented results in the absence of meaningful options for most students. Coordination is required and can be achieved.

NOTES

1. UECU Begins High School–College University Without Walls Program," Union for Experimenting Colleges and Universities, Antioch College, Yellow Springs, Ohio, Jan. 30, 1974.

2. George Gallup, *Fifth Annual Survey of the Public's Attitudes Toward the Public Schools* (Princeton, N.J.: Public Opinion Surveys, Inc., 1973), pp. 21–22.

CHAPTER 8

Work/Study Programs as Educational Alternatives

Recommendation No. 15

The Task Force views work/study programs as a way to teach the inseparable relationship of education and work. Therefore, it is recommended that all types of work/study programs in schools be expanded to give all high-school-age students the opportunity to develop marketable skills prior to graduation.

American high schools, as the report of the National Commission on the Reform of Secondary Education points out, are forever being subjected to traumatic changes in mission.[1] Presently, the schools are facing still another change in mission—a return to the demand that students leaving school must have marketable skills.

The Task Force makes two observations concerning the concept of marketable skills. First, its members believe that these marketable skills should not be so job specific that they become obsolete with new technology. For example, schools should teach interested young people various word-processing skills and not focus exclusively on shorthand. Secondly, they believe that the truly marketable skills often involve such general abilities as problem solving, information retrieval, creative-thinking and assessment-evaluation processes—rather than packing, shipping, and ringing the cash register.

The return of emphasis on marketable skills grows from increasing public realization that a sizable proportion of high school graduates are not equipped for post-secondary vocational training or for job entry. The result of these pressures has been an overwhelming concern for career education.

In 1972, the *Fourth Annual Survey of the Public's Attitudes Toward the Public Schools* indicated that 44 percent of the general public thought the most important goal of education was "to get better jobs."[2] In 1973, this general attitude toward the career potential of public education was investigated by additional survey questioning. The 1973 survey indicated that 90 percent of the general public and 90 percent of professional educators felt that public schools should ". . . give more emphasis to a study of trades, professions, and businesses to help students decide on their careers."[3] The results of the National Commission on the Reform of Secondary Education's nationwide goals survey involving superintendents, principals, teachers, students, and parents indicated 62 percent viewed occupational competence as an important goal of high school education.[4] A national survey conducted by a research associate in the National Institute of Education recently asked respondents to rank six goals of secondary education. The results indicated that occupational competence was ranked number one.[5]

In short, there appears to be a reversal of the attitude recently held by a majority of publics that "programs in occupational education are for someone else's children." Evidence to support this notion is found in the widespread introduction of career education programs from kindergarten through grade 12. This change in perspective places a tremendous burden on school systems whose programs for occupational competence are already inadequate (according to industrial standards) and whose financial resources are becoming increasingly insufficient. The Task Force believes that a viable means of meeting this new demand is through dramatic expansion of the work/study and cooperative programs now operating in many high schools. Public support for allowing students to make greater use of educational opportunities outside the school is also increasing. The previously cited Gallup Survey for 1972 showed 56 percent of the general public and 72 percent of professional educators approved of using outside opportunities. The 1973 Survey, also previously cited, reported increases to 62 percent for the general public and 80 percent for professional educators.

An Overview of Work/Study and Cooperative Programs

A DEFINITION

Work/study is the traditional term for describing programs in which high school students attend regular classes for a portion of each day and spend the remainder of the day in paid employment with an organization that supports their training and development. A major component of work/study is cooperative education, integrating classroom experiences and practical work experiences in a planned educational program. The employment part of the program may be related to the student's choice of careers or may be considered as a broader developmental learning experience.

Existing Types of Work/Study and Cooperative Programs

VOCATIONAL-COOP EDUCATIONAL PROGRAMS

Cooperative programs are planned and supervised jointly by the school and the employer. Part of the student's time in school is spent in job-related instruction. Work periods and school attendance may take place on alternate half-days, days, weeks, or other periods of time. Students are paid for their work; state plans usually stipulate that they must not displace other employees who perform such work. Programs are open to high school juniors and seniors or students sixteen years of age and older. Some examples of cooperative programs are:

- *Distributive Education*—a cooperative program in which concentration is on the development of skills and attitudes for selling and merchandising
- *Cooperative Office Education*—a cooperative program concerned with developing those skills and attitudes necessary for clerical and other office work
- *Cooperative Health Occupations*—a cooperative program designed for the development of skills and attitudes for employment in hospitals, clinics, or other medically oriented work places
- *Diversified Cooperative Training*—a cooperative program designed to treat a wide variety of job opportunities and career choices (It does not focus on any particular career cluster.)
- *Cooperative Child Care Services*—a cooperative program concerned with preparing students for employment in child care centers, handicapped children's clinics, and other agencies where young children are involved

General Work/Study Programs

General work/study programs have traditionally been aimed at non-college-bound students and potential dropouts. They have been reasonably successful in keeping students in high schools by providing opportunities for financial assistance through work. While many programs may have additional goals such as improving students' attitudes toward school and work, few offer related classroom instruction or intensified training. The Task Force believes that schools participating in general work/study programs should incorporate related courses in the curriculum and should encourage participation of college-bound students.

Performance Contracting

Performance contracting is an arrangement by which businesses or industries enter contractual agreements with schools or school systems to develop certain skills in students for a predetermined fee. The Task Force considers such programs to be a worthwhile project for providing work experiences and on-the-job training in highly specialized areas such as watchmaking and repair. The number of students desiring training in such occupations is usually small, requiring few training slots. Payment by the school or school system to the training employer is usually prorated by the extent to which the specified skills are developed and demonstrated. Funds are derived from regular budgetary sources.

Job-Entry Programs

Job entry is the most recent example of educational programs involving compensated work on a full-time basis as a means of earning high school credits. At this writing, the Task

Force knows of one state (Florida) which has embarked on such a project. The program is open to high school seniors between the ages of sixteen and twenty-one who have completed other specific course requirements, have studied a vocational course related to the chosen work area or can demonstrate a degree of competency in it, and are willing to sign an agreement as an employee-trainee. Students are supervised by a full-time coordinator and are awarded one Carnegie Unit for each 288 hours of work on the job. This arrangement permits students to earn five such credits toward graduation in an academic year. Students completing the program may enter regular employment or pursue further training at the post-secondary level.

Work Experience Programs

All of the programs mentioned above restrict participation to high school juniors and/or seniors sixteen years of age and older. Many states also operate work experience programs for fourteen- and fifteen-year-old students. These programs provide for two hours of job-related instruction within the school each day. One hour is for general instruction in a large-group situation. The second hour involves instruction and counseling specifically related to each student's job and is conducted in small groups. The programs are basically exploratory in nature and are frequently aimed at dropout-prone students identified at the junior high school level. On-the-job training is an integral part of the program.

Strengths of Cooperative Programs

Of the programs previously discussed, the cooperative educational models seem to hold the most promise for developing marketable skills that are career oriented. Their particular strengths are:

• They contain provisions for job-related instruction within the schools.

• Students receive career counseling.

• Opportunities are provided for students to work in jobs that coincide with career plans, offer some level of responsibility, and afford a high degree of satisfaction.

• The distributive cooperative programs offer participants club activities which provide extensive opportunities for social growth, competition on state, district, regional, and national levels, as well as opportunities to develop and exercise leadership.

• Job placement is an integral part of all programs.

Advantages of Work/Study and Cooperative Programs

There are advantages for student-trainees, the schools, and employer-trainers in well-planned and executed work/study programs.

ADVANTAGES FOR STUDENTS

1. *Increased Relevance in Education.* Students are given a basis for finding increased meaning in classroom studies because theories and principles learned can be immediately tested and applied to work assignments.

2. *Expanded Opportunities for Career Exploration.* Students are provided opportunities to explore several possible occupational choices within the limits of their aptitudes and interests as they acquire information relative to job requirements, educational requirements, and possibilities for advancement. Such exploratory opportunities are beneficial both to students who are not committed to a career choice and to those who have made choices that seem unwise after exploration.

3. *Increased Maturity and Personal Growth.* Students' maturation processes are accelerated as they adjust to job demands and become increasingly independent of adult supervision and control.

4. *Improved Communication and Understanding Between Students and Adults.* Students are provided opportunities to work with members of other age groups to eliminate the artificial separation that exists today between adolescents and adults. Communications are improved and each group better understands both the differences and the similarities between them.

5. *Increased Probability of Employment After Graduation.* Students in these programs gain certain advantages for regular job placement over students who have not participated in work/study. Even though additional training may be required, the initial skills already developed help adolescents secure regular or part-time employment.[6]

ADVANTAGES FOR SCHOOLS

1. *Program Expansion.* Work/study programs permit schools to expand career development programs through community resources, both human and physical, without burdensome additional outlays of funds.

2. *Faculty Awareness Is Improved.* Teachers are helped to keep abreast of latest developments in various specialized areas in which their students are or may become involved.

3. *Improved School-Community Relations.* Because of the close cooperation between schools and communities in effective work/study programs, the two become more closely allied in other endeavors, and each gains a better understanding of the goals and problems of the other.

4. *More Efficient Use of School Facilities and Financial Resources.* With a sizable proportion of student populations out of the buildings for part of the day, more flexible patterns

of grouping for instruction are possible. And with the soaring costs of training equipment, it is far more economical to utilize industrial equipment for training programs. Furthermore, the instruction students receive from experienced workmen is more valuable than that received from teachers who may lack on-the-job experience.

ADVANTAGES FOR EMPLOYER-TRAINERS

1. *Recruitment of Future Employees.* In addition to the chance to interest promising students in a particular field of work, the employer-trainer can screen employee-trainees for their desirability as permanent employees. If students accept employment after graduation, they will not need the extensive training normally required by new employees.

2. *Opportunities to Contribute to Educational Improvement.* Because of their day-to-day contact with students in the work place, employers can make a public contribution in assessing the quality of educational programs. Most employers enjoy this chance to provide a public service.

Potential Constraints to Program Expansion

There are several potential constraints to expansion of work/study programs. These must be carefully studied and analyzed in terms of each local situation and, where necessary, special dispensations must be sought. Some constraints are treated in the next chapter and are applicable here as well. Others are as follows:

• *Legislation.* In some states laws may inhibit program expansion. Where this occurs, waivers can be requested through the state department of education. Sometimes waivers will permit temporary operation until existing legislation can be amended or enabling legislation passed.

• *Labor Unions.* Labor unions can become a serious constraint where student placement is sought in unionized occupations. But unions are also concerned about quality education for youth. Harold Gibbons, vice-president of the International Brotherhood of Teamsters, urged educators to see that the following criteria are met:

> A. Union leadership thoroughly understands the purposes of the programs.
> B. Union representatives are included in planning, monitoring, and evaluating the programs.
> C. Union membership is convinced that the programs do not represent attempts to provide cheap labor or to displace them from jobs.[7]

In several career training programs visited by the Task Force, the unions have been quite receptive to involvement in the educational process. Many students hold membership in labor unions.

• *Liability and Insurance.* State liability and insurance laws must be carefully checked with the insurance commissioner and compliance achieved. In many states, students who are paid employees of businesses and industries are covered by Workmen's Compensation. In instances where this is not the case, schools must ensure that students are covered under a twenty-four hour school insurance plan or that parents carry adequate coverage in hospitalization and accident insurance. This factor must be included in the agreement the students and their parents make with the school and training agency.

COLLEGE ADMISSIONS

As students opt for work/study programs, they must be advised of requirements for college entrance, and their records must be constantly monitored to assure that requirements are being met if college attendance is anticipated. Participation in work/study programs must not foreclose the option of higher education.

Business, Industry, and Labor Union
Involvement in Work/Study Programs

Most businessmen, industrialists, and union officials realize they must depend upon the educational enterprise for future trained personnel. Their personnel needs include the entire gamut of jobs—from management to research-and-development scientists and engineers through nonscientific personnel for specialized departmental duties such as traffic management, job evaluation, and accounting, as well as skilled, semiskilled, and unskilled workers. All these employees can better adjust to job situations and shorten the period before advancement if they have acquired a basic understanding of actual working conditions.

The last few years have seen encouraging progress in collaboration between education and industry. Many corporations, acting individually, are already involved in jointly sponsored activities with one or more schools and in providing supplementary educational materials. Much of this effort, however, is isolated on both sides of the partnership; too often the cooperation merely reflects a request from a single teacher or school to a single firm.

Close cooperation between the two communities, however, is both desirable and possible. Among those urging it is the national Chamber of Commerce which has long been disturbed by what its officers regard as bias against programs that prepare youth for specific occupational pursuits.[8] Because the policies of the national chamber serve as guidelines for local chambers, almost every urban school system has at its disposal the nucleus of a school-community coordinating group.

Four programs established with the help of chambers of commerce are especially interesting:

• *Dallas' Alliance for Progress.* The Dallas school superintendent, addressing the local chamber, challenged its membership to help education benefit from the discipline and know-how of the business world. The challenge was accepted, and a committee of the chamber conducted a one-year study of seven major areas of school district management. The resulting recommendations served as a guidebook to greater efficiency for the school system and cemented a mutually beneficial alliance between business and education in Dallas. The chamber also established a task force on vocational opportunity which takes an active part in the district's career education program. A full-time coordinator paid by the chamber works as liaison between local businessmen and school administrators.[9]

• *Detroit Industries as Partners of High Schools.* Industrial and commercial firms collaborate with public schools to make high school experiences more relevant to the needs of students. The companies make available to faculties and students a variety of materials, equipment, and staff to improve and motivate learning. Placement in permanent employment upon graduation is an integral part of these programs.[10]

• *Boston's Flexible Campus.* Directly sponsored by the Greater Boston Chamber of Commerce, this program permits students to leave their regular classrooms for expanded learning opportunities in their community. The students can choose special mini-courses taught by volunteer businessmen in such areas as construction, accounting, and economics; they can learn through on-the-job, nonpaid work experiences offered by businesses, or they can utilize other resources in the city for off-campus learning experiences. There are seventy-two companies participating in the program and twenty-eight of them release employees to teach courses in the schools—some for limited periods, others for the full year.[11]

• *Portland, Oregon's IPAR—Metropolitan Schools Pilot Project.* The Portland Chamber of Commerce is one of the participants in Institute for Public Affairs Research–Metropolitan

Schools Pilot Project. IPAR was first organized to help high school students understand economics by contact with speakers from outside the school. One of its goals is to minimize the traditional barriers between the academic and the working worlds.

Though partnership between education and business is essential and must be encouraged, the Task Force insists that the alliance remain limited. Work/study programs are complements to rather than replacements for programs and experiences offered in the high school. American schools do not exist solely to train young people to fit predetermined slots or to meet the specific manpower needs of American industry.

NOTES

1. *The Reform of Secondary Education: A Report to the Public and the Profession* (New York: McGraw-Hill Book Company, 1973), p. 9.

2. George Gallup, *Fourth Annual Survey of the Public's Attitudes Toward the Public Schools* (Princeton, N.J.: Public Opinion Surveys, Inc., spring 1972), p. 9.

3. George Gallup, *Fifth Annual Survey of the Public's Attitudes Toward the Public Schools* (Princeton, N.J.: Public Opinion Surveys, Inc., spring 1973), p. 20.

4. *The Reform of Secondary Education: A Report to the Public and the Profession* (New York: McGraw-Hill Book Company, 1973), p. 187.

5. Paul T. Hill, "Public Views on the Objectives of Secondary Education: The Results of a Survey" (an abstract, November 1973), p. 5.

6. President's Science Advisory Committee, *Youth: Transition to Adulthood* (Washington, D.C.: U.S. Government Printing Office, 1973), p. 130.

7. Remarks made by Harold Gibbons, vice-president of the International Brotherhood of Teamsters Union, to Task Force '74 members at a meeting in Louisville, Kentucky, Dec. 18, 1973.

8. Urban Action Clearing House, *Dallas' New Alliance for Progress* (Washington, D.C.: Chamber of Commerce of the United States, 1970).

9. Ibid.

10. Urban Action Clearing House, *Detroit Industries Become Partners of Core-City High Schools* (Washington, D.C.: Chamber of Commerce of the United States, 1968).

11. Urban Strategy Center, *Boston's Flexible Campus Program* (Washington, D.C.: Chamber of Commerce of the United States, 1972).

CHAPTER 9

Youth Service Programs as Educational Alternatives

Recommendation No. 16

The Task Force believes that all high schools should encourage and sponsor extensive youth service programs involving a variety of community and governmental agencies. Therefore, it is recommended that individual class schedules in high schools be designed in such a way as to provide time during the school day for students to leave the building and perform youth services in their communities.

During the past several years, American adolescents have shown increasing concern about social problems that remain unsolved and community needs that go unmet. Many of the most committed students have been spurred to action. While some of the most publicized of these actions have produced negative results, many more of the quieter efforts have made a desirable difference for the students and their society.

The very real concern, high motivation, and enormous energy of high school students are potentially great assets for society. But these assets usually remain potential rather than real because there is no identifiable group to coordinate adolescent efforts. Schools, as socializing agencies, are the natural centers for such planning and should accept the responsibility.

Today, many schools give no more than casual encouragement to youth service programs. A prime example is the "Candy Stripers" program operated by most hospitals. This program uses eleventh- and twelfth-grade high school girls in a variety of necessary activities within the hospitals. In spite of the large number of students participating, schools usually provide no released time for this work and do not give credit for it. Students can serve only after school and on weekends. This restriction virtually excludes those students who must work for pay when not in school or who have specific family responsibilities.

Schools which have systematically incorporated volunteer work into their educational programs have found the results encouraging. These programs also provide additional opportunities for students to develop marketable skills while acquiring expertise in human relations and understanding of social responsibilities.

An Overview of Youth Service Programs

DEFINITION

Youth service programs are educational options that involve students in the activities of social agencies for no remuneration. The programs can be initiated by the high schools or by the social agencies. Supervision by school personnel is the customary format. The programs are usually designed so that students further their education while performing services for others. The emphasis is on helping others. By definition, youth service activities are responsible and productive, introducing the roles, constraints, and demands of adulthood.

PURPOSES OF YOUTH SERVICE PROGRAMS

The purposes of youth service programs are:

• To offer high school students "true life" experiences as part of their educational program

• To encourage students in the development of emotional and intellectual commitments to the solution of social problems

• To help youth undertake responsible roles in society and grow in maturity

• To help students become contributing and productive citizens

• To provide a service to local institutions

Advantages of Youth Service Programs

FOR STUDENTS

As in work/study programs, students participating in youth service programs acquire skills that are in demand and a greater understanding of themselves. In addition, work for social agencies helps in the development of empathy for others at all age levels.

FOR SCHOOLS

School-community relations improve greatly as schools become more active and positive forces in their communities. Educational resources are expanded by the addition of agency personnel and facilities; and the integration of course work and community service adds relevance to the curriculum.

FOR SOCIAL AGENCIES

Alienation from and discontent with adults are diminished among youth who have a stake in community affairs, increasing both present and future support for the agencies. Moreover, the work done by the students genuinely does improve the quality of performance by the social agencies.

Agencies Offering Opportunities for Service Activities

Among the social agencies that would be willing to enter into cooperative arrangements with schools are the following:

CRIPPLED CHILDREN'S CLINICS

Crippled Children's Clinics offer experience for students contemplating physical therapy or counseling as a career.

DAY CARE CENTERS

The growth of day care centers extends the possibility of volunteer activities. Youth services in the centers are complementary to in-school courses in human development and child care. A few high schools run day care centers for their neighborhoods, with students as key "employees."

GOVERNMENT AGENCIES

Students enrolled in government and political science courses gain field experiences by volunteering to work in welfare offices, parks departments, courts and court-related agencies, etc.

HOME DEMONSTRATION AGENTS

Students enrolled in homemaking can volunteer to work with home demonstration agents. Activities include interior decorating, budgeting, shopping, and cooking.

HOSPITALS

Volunteer work in hospitals has great appeal for some high school students. The previously mentioned "Candy Stripers" represent an excellent model for hospital service. Activities which can be performed by students are:

- Serving as nurses' aides
- Operating telephone switchboards
- Staffing the information desk
- Serving as floor hosts or hostesses
- Transporting patients to x-ray and treatment rooms
- Working in the hospitality shop
- Manning a cheer cart with articles from the hospitality shop
- Working in the hospital kitchen as dieticians' assistants
- Delivering flowers to patients' rooms and subsequently caring for flowers
- Visiting with patients who seldom receive other visitors
- Babysitting with young children while their parents visit patients

HOUSING AUTHORITY

Building maintenance on publicly owned housing offers practical experience for students in industrial arts and the building construction trades.

"MEALS ON WHEELS" AND FEDERALLY SUBSIDIZED BREAKFAST PROGRAMS

Students help prepare balanced diets and hot meals for the aged and for young children in elementary and junior high schools.

MENTAL HEALTH UNITS

Volunteer work in mental health centers provides valuable field experiences for students studying or planning to study psychology.

NURSING HOMES

Nursing homes need all the help they can get. In addition to the hospital work outlined above, volunteers at nursing homes may be engaged in:

- Talking with elderly people
- Pushing wheelchairs
- Managing portable libraries and helping patients in the selection of reading materials
- Planning and arranging various forms of entertainment, such as group singing
- Playing games with the elderly

Such volunteer activities obviously contribute to the mastery of a sociology unit on aging. Many students will some day have to manage some of these situations themselves, giving these activities special relevance to their future.

PUBLIC HEALTH FACILITIES

Public health facilities in most communities offer a number of activities in which high school students can volunteer to participate. Volunteers may help the scientists of the ecological control unit, sanitary engineers, food service inspectors, water supply technicians, etc. In some cities, students have been used as assistants in V.D. clinics, on drug "hot lines," and in immunization departments.

SENIOR CITIZEN CENTERS

The growth of senior citizen centers is an emerging new phenomenal movement which could utilize many young people.

SCHOOLS

Elementary, junior high, and senior high schools offer numerous opportunities for students to provide tutorial services. Tutoring may involve older students helping younger students, peers helping each other, and even younger students helping older students. Often the experience is even more valuable for the tutor than for the tutee; ancient wisdom in education holds that the best way to learn a subject is to teach it. Tutoring is obviously the first priority service activity for students who are considering teaching as a career.

Constraints to Program Implementation

The constraints discussed in the chapter on work/study programs also apply to youth service programs. An additional difficulty may be the cost of student transportation to and from the social agencies. These costs must not be burdensome. If the programs are effective, the agencies should be willing to help arrange transportation.

Graduation requirements, college admission, scheduling, grading and credentialing, and racial isolation are concerns here as well as in the previous chapters. Keeping them in mind will not resolve them easily—but neglecting them will be tantamount to a collapse of effective youth service programs.

School-sponsored volunteer programs that provide services for others are efficient methods by which high schools can increase the options available to students. The Task Force realizes that not all schools will have access to all of the agencies listed in this chapter. However, almost every community provides public services that can be the locus of a program, and schools that make the effort will soon find volunteer activity an apparently natural adjunct to the formal curriculum.

CHAPTER 10

Planning Processes for Alternative Programs

Recommendation No. 17

The Task Force believes extensive planning is essential to the success of any educational change. Therefore, it is recommended that high schools contemplating alternative programs should acquire the requisite skills needed to develop a planning calendar that leads logically to the date of implementation.

Recommendation No. 18

The Task Force believes that any alternative program should demonstrate its ability to achieve expected outcomes at least as well as the traditional high school program. Therefore, it is recommended that districts planning alternative programs develop comprehensive evaluation plans which include written comprehensive examinations, demonstration of minimum competencies, completion of objectives, and fulfillment of school-student contractual agreements.

Recommendation No. 19

The Task Force believes that work/study and youth service programs require input from advisory councils to maximize the use of both human and physical community resources. Therefore, it is recommended that such advisory councils be created to participate in planning, monitoring, and evaluating the programs.

In establishing alternative programs for American high schools, the administration and faculty must consider their physical plant; faculty, parent, student, and community attitudes; and the availability and suitability of community resources. Alternative programs are more likely to succeed when each school develops its own specific plans to meet the needs and interests of its own students.

The Task Force proposes, in the following pages, a systematic process by which a school system can develop a comprehensive program of alternatives. Its members believe that the process provides for the involvement of participants and encourages the rational planning necessary for success. Even when the enthusiasm of teachers and students makes it possible to shorten the process, all the major steps outlined below should be taken.

Every planning model has problems. The careful long-term planning described in the following pages must be monitored to assure planning is done with people rather than for them.

Any school planning group must address and deal with administrative organization, learning strategies, curricular structures, and personal characteristics of staff members. The following are bases to be touched:

I. *Administrative Organization*

A. Check policies and standards of regional accrediting association and ascertain whether projected program complies.

B. Check state statutes for inhibiting legislation.

C. School board policies and administrative regulations must be studied and revisions sought where necessary.

D. If the program to be implemented involves placing students in union shops, cooperation of the union leadership and membership must be obtained.

E. If the program involves students in off-campus training experiences, liability insurance laws must be carefully examined. Where students are not covered by Workmen's Compensation, the administration must ensure that students are covered under a twenty-four-hour school insurance plan or that parents carry adequate coverage in hospitalization and accident insurance.

F. Administration must determine how funds are to be reallocated and how much additional financing will be necessary to pay for staffing and instructional materials. The philosophy must be that funds follow the student.

G. Procedures must be developed to ensure that the staff and student body are broadly representative of the ethnic composition of the school.

II. *Learning Strategies*

A. The administration and teaching staff must determine the extent to which the following selected learning strategies will be applied:

1. Teacher-pupil contact
2. Group interaction
3. Learning packages, commercially available or locally prepared
4. Independent study
5. Unstructured experience
6. Multi-age grouping
7. Tutorials

III. *Curriculum Structure*

A. Learning strategies must be matched to programs.

B. A variety of alternative approaches to grading and awarding of credits must be established.

C. The curriculum must be structured to ensure that all students can enroll in courses that will meet college entrance requirements. Provisions must also be included for meeting local and state graduation requirements.

D. If community involvement programs are adopted, students must be assisted in arranging their schedules so that a balance is maintained between the number of students in the building and the number of students outside the building at any given time. In Michigan, the goal now under consideration is a schedule that places at least 65 percent of the high school eleventh and twelfth grades in learning activities outside the high school buildings for 50 percent of the time.

E. A system for continuous evaluation must be devised.

IV. *Personal Characteristics of Staff Members*

A. The success of any educational program depends mostly on the characteristics of the people on the staff. Administrators will have to develop meaningful criteria for selection and assignment of staff to optional programs. Among the attributes to be considered are:

1. Personality
2. Knowledge of how students learn
3. Knowledge of subject matter
4. Skill in utilizing a variety of instructional approaches
5. Skill in human relationships
6. Skill in motivational techniques
7. Skill in managing the learning experiences
8. The ability to respect students
9. The ability to communicate effectively with students, parents, and peers

Having dealt adequately with the above, the administrative

team should be in a position to write a final proposal for alternative programs to be presented to the school board.

CALENDAR

The calendar which follows on pages 102 to 106 lists most of the tasks that must be performed and the responsible agent. The suggested timelines are based on the assumption that the alternative programs are to be implemented in September 1976.

Cautionary Notes

RACIAL ISOLATION

School systems implementing alternative programs must devise a selection system that will prevent racial isolation. Allowing parents and students to choose programs without adequate safeguards can result in students being classified or separated according to ethnic origin, economic status, or parental education. Although each program should roughly reflect the racial and ethnic composition of the entire school district, certain multi-cultural programs may produce heavier concentrations of minority students. In such cases, the school district must carefully monitor the program to avoid racial isolation. Segregation of students may be illegal even though accomplished through the offering of multi-cultural alternatives.

A prime example is the Berkeley, California experiment with alternatives under a grant from the U.S. Office of Education. Two alternatives formerly operated (Black House with a Black enrollment and Casa de la Raza with a Chicano enrollment) were found to be in violation of Title VI of the Federal Education Act. In June 1973, the district agreed to close the two programs in order to maintain federal funding.[1]

DATE	TASK	AGENT
June 1975	Develop a preliminary proposal for alternative programs to be presented to school board for approval. The proposal should include necessary changes in board policies and administrative regulations, areas in which the board should seek changes in legislation, if any, and any additional finances that might be needed for planning and implementation.	Superintendent, and/or his staff, and/or school personnel
July 1975	Present proposal to school board for approval and appoint, organize, and orient planning committee.	Superintendent and his staff
August 1975	Conduct preliminary studies. The preliminary studies should yield sufficient background information for the planning committee to sell the value of multiple alternatives to parents, students, and teachers.	Planning committee
September 1975	Make extensive efforts to inform general public. The general public must be informed through open meetings within the district and use of radio, television, and newspapers.	Planning committee
October 1975	Conduct needs assessment. The assessment instrument should elicit information from parents and students relative to the kinds of educational programs desired, educational goals, and expected outcomes. The desired degrees of structure and control should also be indicated.	Planning subcommittee
November 1975	Identify resources and constraints. Physical facilities at the schools must be surveyed to determine the amount of space available, the	Planning subcommittee

number of alternatives that can be adequately housed, and the approximate amount of space which can be allocated to each program. Community resources, both human and material, must be surveyed to determine the approximate number of persons who can serve as volunteers in the school; the number of persons who can be used as consultants; the number of businesses and industries that will accept student trainees; and the number of businesses and industries that will make personnel available on released time to teach classes in the school. This information is necessary for determining how extensively the community at large can be included in the educational program.

Probable constraints to full implementation of programs must also be identified and resolved. A few examples follow:

Regional Accreditation. Policies and requirements of the applicable regional association must be checked and, where necessary, concessions requested.

Labor Unions. Where the programs involve labor unions, their support and cooperation must be solicited.

College Admissions. Entrance requirements for area colleges must be checked to be sure that all programs meet specified criteria for admission.

Graduation Requirements. Care must be taken to ensure that all students meet requirements for graduation. (Some state and local requirements may have to be waived or revised.)

DATE	TASK	AGENT
	Liability and Insurance. State liability and insurance laws must be checked and plans for compliance developed in cases where programs involve off-campus experiences.	Planning committee
December 1975	Develop tentative list of alternatives. Based on information from needs assessment and identified resources, a tentative list of options should be prepared.	Planning subcommittee
January 1976	Survey students, parents, and teachers on preferences among options. Alternatives should also be indicated.	Planning subcommittee
February 1976	Determine final list of options. On the basis of first preferences, a final list of available options should be made. Also, budgetary allocations should be approved along with the plan for general staffing,	Superintendent and his staff
	Final proposal submitted to the superintendent and to the board for approval.	
March 1976	Preregister students for 1977–78 school year and appoint a task force for program implementation.	Planning committee
April thru June 1976	Unit planning. Program planning for each optional unit must involve students, parents, teachers, and community representatives. Planning should cover the following: I. Overall goals and objectives II. Curriculum	Task force

III. Space utilization
IV. Performance expectation
V. Flexible grading and credentialing
  A. Each program should have a flexible grading and credentialing structure containing a variety of options:
    1. Grading
      a. letter grades
      b. pass/fail
      c. credit/no credit
      d. written evaluation
    2. Credentialing
      a. Carnegie Units
      b. units of work
      c. meeting learning objectives
      d. comprehensive examinations
      e. demonstration of minimum competency
      f. fulfillment of individual contract
VI. Scheduling must be flexible; however, it must reflect the best utilization of facilities and resources
VII. Decision-making process (how much student and parent involvement)
VIII. Pupil personnel services
IX. Program evaluation
X. Teacher evaluation

DATE	TASK	AGENT
July 1976	Finalize plans for implementation.	Task force
August 1976	Orient students, parents, and general public.	Task force
September 1976	Implement alternative programs.	Task force
November 1976	Conduct first evaluation of alternative programs. Evaluation of educational programs is considered crucial to program effectiveness. Thus, optional programs must be continually evaluated as a measure of effectiveness and a basis for program revision. It is vital that students, parents, teachers, and lay citizens participate in the evaluative process. The purposes of program evaluation are as follows: I. To provide for program improvement which in turn relates to the process of continuous planning II. To establish the program's credibility with a variety of publics III. To provide a base for identifying those options that are effective and those that are not	Planning committee

FRAGMENTATION

Care must be taken to ensure that the various programs do not become detached from the school. Certain physical facilities and resources utilized by all students can serve as an appropriate focus for the corporate life of the school.

ACADEMIC SOFTNESS

Academic standards must be maintained. Even though students participate in the selection of their learning activities, they must be required to establish and maintain standards of quality and performance.

LEGAL PROBLEMS

The school board's attorney should be knowledgeable about school law and the various titles of the Civil Rights Act.

AWARDING CREDITS

One of the barriers to the establishment of cooperative programs has been the difficulty of persuading state agencies and regional accrediting associations to accept such service in lieu of academic instruction. If students are to acquire a better understanding of the world of work, particularly as it relates to service organizations, state departments and accrediting associations must be convinced of the validity of different ways to give credit.

EVALUATION

The experimental nature of many alternative programs poses a special problem of evaluation. (1) Their high visibility suggests the need for objective assessment to establish credibility. (2) Their unique nature suggests that they be evaluated in terms of both their own objectives and the common goals of all schools. (3) Their experimental nature cautions against premature judgment.

ESTABLISHMENT OF ADVISORY COUNCILS

Community advisory councils must be organized for work/study and youth service programs. In establishing these councils, school personnel must arrange for representation of all the community agencies involved in the programs.

One of the first functions of such advisory councils should be to develop lists of job titles and job descriptions for prospective students. Another prime function of the advisory council must be participatory planning which should be conducted jointly with school personnel. Although the operation of alternative programs is the responsibility of the schools, monitoring and evaluation of both work/study and youth service programs should be the joint responsibility of school personnel and community representatives.

NOTE

1. Information supplied by Mr. Fred Cioffi, operations officer for the Elementary and Secondary Education Section, Office of Civil Rights, HEW, Washington, D.C.

CHAPTER 11

Recommendations

Recommendation No. 1

The Task Force believes that most communities have individuals and groups who are interested in and have the potential for becoming actively involved in making decisions that affect the nature and future of education. Therefore, it is recommended that local citizens and community groups immediately increase their participation until they are actively involved in forming policies, making decisions, and governing their schools.

Recommendation No. 2

The Task Force recognizes that within a community a widely representative group should be formed to represent a broad mix of values, attitudes, and cultures. Group members should have the opportunity to increase their skills in communication, problem solving, and decision making. Therefore, it is recommended that each state develop methods of ensuring community involvement in all levels of education.

Recommendation No. 3

The Task Force realizes that some formal legal structure will be required if citizen groups are to be permanently established as a force in education. Therefore, it is recommended that each state develop methods to (a) enable community groups to develop and acquire skills in communication, problem solving, and decision making and (b) make available adequate funds to support community involvement in all levels of education.

Recommendation No. 4

The Task Force believes that significant educational change can be accomplished only through the cooperative efforts of educators, students, and citizens. Therefore, it is recommended that educators take the initiative in stimulating citizen involvement in high school reform.

Recommendation No. 5

The Task Force endorses the idea of community school boards for individual schools. Therefore, it is recommended that individual community boards be permitted to participate in the selection of principals, the evaluation of teachers, authorization of programs of instruction, approval of local building plans, etc., within centrally approved budgets. The school district board should therefore be limited to general policy formation, budget preparation, and review.

Recommendation No. 6

The Task Force recognizes that advisory committees must be trained before they can become involved effectively, but insists that this training must not come from the groups or professions which are being advised. Therefore, it is recommended that funds be allocated for external trainers and staff assistants not paid or controlled by local school boards or administrators.

Recommendation No. 7

The Task Force applauds the involvement of business and industry in the education of the nation's youth and seeks its extension. Therefore, it is recommended that the business community accept increased responsibility for helping educators find solutions to some of the problems of the high school.

Recommendation No. 8

The Task Force is aware that there are many decisions which can only be made after completion of negotiations between teacher organizations and school boards, but cautions against the further extension of collective bargaining into areas over which citizens have traditionally exercised control. Therefore, it is recommended that collective bargaining between school boards and teachers be limited to the area of teacher welfare, i.e., salaries, fringe benefits, and grievance procedures.

Recommendation No. 9

The Task Force believes that citizen concern about the privacy of school negotiations which tends to prevent their involvement in many of the negotiated decisions is legitimate and, hopefully, such negotiations will be more open to public review. Therefore, it is recommended that upon the completion of privately conducted negotiations—but prior to the signing of any collective-bargaining agreement—the school board should be required to hold a series of public hearings to allow maximum citizen input before final contract approval.

Recommendation No. 10

The Task Force notes that salary arrangements for middle management are now tied too closely to teachers' salaries, creating a lock-step ratio in salary schedules for teachers and principals. Therefore, it is recommended that school boards recognize the complexities and extreme pressures of the principalship and designate principals and other middle-management groups as members of the management team with compensation determined independently.

Recommendation No. 11

The Task Force realizes that schools will not improve significantly unless individual student rights are balanced with individual student responsibilities to the school and society. Therefore, it is recommended that each high school further the opportunity for citizen involvement by establishing a committee composed of students, teachers, administrators, and community representatives broadly chosen for the purpose of identifying, posting, and widely disseminating in the school's literature the responsibilities students are expected to accept.

Recommendation No. 12

The Task Force believes that a sense of these responsibilities is best acquired when students have the opportunity to assume responsibility as a way of learning the relationship between actions and consequences. An interdisciplinary approach is suggested which will place particular emphasis on the areas of English and social studies. Therefore, it is recommended that substantial state and federal resources be allocated for research and development designed to implement a new focus on student responsibilities, utilizing an interdisciplinary curricular approach.

Recommendation No. 13

The Task Force believes that the community college is a viable alternative to the last year of high school for many students. Therefore, it is recommended that action be taken by state departments of education to facilitate and coordinate the movement of high school students into the community colleges and to eliminate the "battle for bodies" now being waged between high school and community college personnel.

Recommendation No. 14

The Task Force urges school districts to move toward a systemwide range of alternatives responsive to the needs of all students. Therefore, it is recommended that school boards and superintendents take steps to coordinate the efforts of principals, teachers, citizens, and students in the development of alternative programs so that the fragmentation of current efforts may be replaced by systemwide planning.

Recommendation No. 15

The Task Force views work/study programs as a way to teach the inseparable relationship of education and work. Therefore, it is recommended that all types of work/study programs in schools be expanded to give all high-school-age students the opportunity to develop marketable skills prior to graduation.

Recommendation No. 16

The Task Force believes that all high schools should encourage and sponsor extensive youth service programs involving a variety of community and governmental agencies. Therefore, it is recommended that individual class schedules in high schools be designed in such a way as to provide time during the school day for students to leave the building and perform youth services in their communities.

Recommendation No. 17

The Task Force believes extensive planning is essential to the success of any educational change. Therefore, it is recommended that high schools contemplating alternative programs should acquire the requisite skills needed to develop a planning calendar that leads logically to the date of implementation.

Recommendation No. 18

The Task Force believes that any alternative program should demonstrate its ability to achieve expected outcomes at least as well as the traditional high school program. Therefore, it is recommended that districts planning alternative programs develop comprehensive evaluation plans which include written comprehensive examinations, demonstration of minimum competencies, completion of objectives, and fulfillment of school-student contractual agreements.

Recommendation No. 19

The Task Force believes that work/study and youth service programs require input from advisory councils to maximize the use of both human and physical community resources. Therefore, it is recommended that such advisory councils be created to participate in planning, monitoring, and evaluating the programs.

Memoranda of Dissent

Page 3, Recommendation No. 1—By Owen B. Kiernan

The several references to governance of schools, veto rights, and full managerial power in this chapter may prove to be somewhat misleading to John Q. Citizen. The Task Force has selected language lacking in specificity and tangentially vague in other references. There can be no debate on the absolute necessity of broadening the base of participation in school affairs or making citizen involvement truly meaningful. The problem arises when all citizens are assigned quarterbacking roles and the issue of accountability is left hanging. Regardless of the number participating in policy formulation in a democratic society, at some point an individual or agency must be charged with final responsibility and accountability. Where this has not been done, battles over the ultimate authority for programs have contributed to confusion and chaos in the school system. Tragically, the person who really gets short-changed in this control warfare is the student. "Full managerial power" as included in this report is not a commodity that can be handed out promiscuously, but in no way should the delegation of final authority diminish true citizen involvement.

Page 20, Alienation column, lines 15-17—By Owen B. Kiernan

On a related matter, I must take exception to the allegation that educators have by "clever and subtle (PR slick approach)" means manipulated the public. There is no hard evidence that any such approach has been or is currently in use. Granted that an enterprise of such magnitude is bound to include a few unethical characters, it constitutes a disservice to the profession to suggest that citizens and educators generally are not members of an effective partnership.

Page 35, Recommendation No. 8—By Allan A. Glatthorn

Perhaps it is at this place in the report that I can best register my objections to what I consider the anti-teacher-organization bias of all sections dealing with teacher-board negotiations. The report seems to undervalue the progress achieved by teacher organizations and to cast those organizations into the role of a self-serving obstructionist force. Such a characterization would not seem borne out by the facts as I know them and at the least would seem to exacerbate the adversarial relationships which the report itself decries.

I take particular exception to Recommendation No. 8. It seems totally unrealistic to believe that the complex matter of deciding which issues are legitimate ones for negotiation can be settled by a pronouncement such as this.

I feel that the Task Force would have made a more positive impact in this critical area of collective bargaining for professionals if it had recommended a national study of the problem, involving all the constituencies with a vested interest in the outcome. Such a study might have produced some new approaches by which professionals, parents, and school boards could resolve legitimate differences without the negative effects of prolonged strikes.

Page 36, Recommendation No. 10—By Allan A. Glatthorn

This recommendation is too simplistic and totally ill-advised. It recommends that principals be designated "members of the management team" and that their salaries then be set "independently." Such a recommendation would leave principals at the mercy of school boards and superintendents, rendering them even more impotent than they are now.

Principals and other members of "middle management" have a legitimate right to organize, as legislatures and the courts have recognized, and through such organizations to protect their rights to secure due process, to maintain their professional authority and independence, and to bargain for adequate compensation. One way of securing adequate compensation is through indexing; it seems unwise to reject such an approach.

Pages 41-42, Principals and Collective Bargaining—By Owen B. Kiernan

To suggest that principals must disassociate themselves from management and/or become adjuncts of teacher unions is to miss the mark completely. In a number of large school systems, collectively negotiated agreements are currently in effect. In several of these, umbrella documents serve the combined administrative and supervisory staffs rather than principals exclusively. However, the National Association of Secondary School Principals vigorously supports independent recognition as well under the following guideline: "If a principal is to carry out administrative responsibilities, if he is to organize and coordinate all school activities, and if he is to be responsible for deploying the school staff to educate students most effectively, he must have reasonable authority to make and implement decisions." By the widest stretch of the imagination these responsibilities could not be met under a teachers' organization adjunct relationship.

Page 45, Recommendation No. 11—By Allan A. Glatthorn

I will use this occasion to register certain objections to the entire section on student responsibilities. First, the section unwisely ignores the social and cultural context. The irresponsibility of our elected officials unwittingly provides a sanction for such behavior on the part of students. Second, the section slights the institutional context. Too many schools are organized and operated in such a way as to reinforce irresponsible behavior: students are too often excluded from the decision-making process and are systematically juvenilized by schools too concerned with their custodial function. Third, the specific recommendations for student responsibility are defined so narrowly and couched in language so monitory that they sound like Boy Scout manuals of the fifties. Finally, the central thrust of the recommendations is concerned too much with obeying authority, an orientation which Kohlberg himself would fix at Level 4. Certainly one of the goals of moral education is to help the adolescent develop a more sophisticated moral judgment.

Page 65, Recommendation No. 13—By Owen B. Kiernan

The "battle for bodies" not only involves high schools and community colleges, but colleges as well. This particular recommendation of the Task Force leaves the impression that collegiate programs should be substituted *in toto* for the high school and that "higher is better." Such conclusions are based on fallacious reasoning which I cannot accept. Each institution should be allowed to do that which it does best. It does not follow that calculus is taught better because the mathematics classroom is located on a higher education campus. Many high schools have achieved outstanding success in offering both short- and long-term electives which may or may not be found in college catalogs. To deny opportunities to broaden secondary school programs is to reduce the effectiveness of one of the nation's most remarkable educational institutions.

The key to successful programs is appropriate cooperation, not competition, between the high school and the college. In my judgment, part-time programs involving both campuses represent the most meaningful breakthrough. Guidelines can be established cooperatively which will return substantial dividends to the participating students. The plan operating in California appears to set the stage for such cooperation, i.e., a principal may recommend up to 15 percent of his eleventh and twelfth graders and the community college president may enroll these students on a part-time basis.

Pages 66–67, "Free" Schools—By Owen B. Kiernan

Most students respond well to what educators have come to describe as the traditional approach, while others require alternatives in nontraditional categories. When the latter are used, it is imperative that a close and effective tie be maintained with the existing secondary school. Responsibility and assessment ultimately must be vested in the local school authorities. Where such a partnership has not been effected, the "free" schools, in spite of glowing publicity, have been short-lived and the record has been one of dismal failure.